D1305858

A TASTE OF
WYOMING

Favorite Recipes from the Cowboy State

by Pamela Sinclair

photography by Paulette Phlipot

foreword by Alyson Hagy

FARCOUNTRY
PRESS
Helena, Montana

ISBN 10: 1-56037-458-6
ISBN 13: 978-1-56037-458-9

© 2008 by Farcountry Press
Text © 2008 by Pamela Sinclair

p. 7: From "Natural Causes" by Lori Van Pelt, © 2002 by Lori Van Pelt, from a book titled
Hot Biscuits. Used by permission of University of New Mexico Press.

p. 24: From *Prairie Soul* by Jeffrey A. Lockwood, © 2004 by Jeffrey A. Lockwood.
Used by permission of Skinner House Books.

p. 58: From *Where Rivers Change Direction* by Mark Spragg, © 1999 by Mark Spragg.
All rights reserved. Used by permission of the author.

p. 85: From *Some Church* (Minneapolis: Milkweed Editions, 2005) by David Romtvedt, © 2005 by
David Romtvedt. Used by permission of Milkweed Editions. (www.milkweed.org)

p. 112: From *The Solace of Open Spaces* by Gretel Ehrlich, © 1985 by Gretel Ehrlich.
Used by permission of Viking Penguin, a division of Penguin Group (USA) Inc.

All rights reserved. This book may not be reproduced in whole or in part by any means (with the
exception of short quotes for the purpose of review) without the permission of the publisher.

For more information on our books, write Farcountry Press, P.O. Box 5630, Helena, MT 59604;
call (800) 821-3874; or visit www.farcountrypress.com.

Library of Congress Cataloging-in-Publication Data

Sinclair, Pamela.
  A taste of Wyoming : favorite recipes from the cowboy state / by Pamela Sinclair ;
  photographs by Paulette Phlipot ; foreword by Alyson Hagy.
       p. cm.
  Includes index.
  ISBN-13: 978-1-56037-458-9
  ISBN-10: 1-56037-458-6
  1. Cookery, American. 2. Cookery--Wyoming. I. Title.
  TX715.S61884 2008
  641.59787--dc22
                                        2007031381
Created, produced, and designed in the United States.
Printed in China.

13 12 11 10 09 08   1 2 3 4 5 6

For everyone who contributed to this book

In the far and mighty West,

Where the crimson sun seeks rest,

There's a growing splendid State that lies above,

On the breast of this great land;

Where the massive Rockies stand,

There's Wyoming young and strong, the State I love!

—verse I of *Wyoming*, official state song
adopted February 15, 1955
lyric by Charles E. Winter
music by George E. Knapp

contents

chapter 1: Breakfast & Brunch

chapter 2: Appetizers & Snacks

chapter 3: Salads & Sides

chapter 4: Soups & Stews

chapter 5: Main Courses

chapter 6: Desserts & Sweet Treats

foreword

by Alyson Hagy

The Taste of Wyoming Is on the Wind

I'm no cook. My idea of food preparation is cramming my mouth full of Absaroka Wilderness raspberries while looking over my shoulder for bears. And I don't usually think of food when I think of Wyoming. Drink, yes. Living at high altitude requires a person to wet her whistle on a regular basis, and human watering holes appear along Wyoming roadways as regularly as oases appear along desert caravan routes. But food? Isn't that what a person wraps in plastic and crams into the pockets of his fishing vest or the glove compartment of her truck (where the dogs can't get to it)? Food is necessary, of course. But out here the repast tends to be portable and unlikely to interfere with the taste of a good cup of coffee or a cold bottle of beer.

Pamela Sinclair, however, has discovered a knotty little Western secret. She has toured our kitchens and our stubborn gardens and our memories. She has listened to the way our stomachs growl before we head off on a brisk hike or after we've spent a twilight hour shoveling snow. She knows our hearts are half-hitched to our dinner plates.

Wyomingites, for instance, spend a darn lot of time talking about how they are going to *get* their food. Elk, deer, pronghorn, pheasant, grouse: I know men who have composed stories the length of Norse sagas on the subject of hunting. And fishing! Don't ever get my neighbor Chuck started on the topic of trout. He is downright operatic on the matter. But folks don't talk much about how they prepare the meat they so strenuously plan to acquire. Is that because, like my Irish mother-in-law, we are bound and determined to cook that flesh until it tastes like shoe leather in the end? Or is it because, as Pamela Sinclair suggests with this mouth-watering amalgam of recipes, those of us from the relatively isolated mountains and plains sometimes have a tendency to keep our deepest pleasures to ourselves?

If on a Winter's Night...

Wyomingites pride themselves on their code of hospitality. We will stop on an icy road and help you change your tire. We will track down your wandering heifers or Labradors. We will return the Christmas decorations that have somehow been blown half a mile east of your yard by our friendly winter winds. We will shoo the rabbits away from your basil plants or lend you an Allen wrench so you can fix your bike on the trail. But will we feed you? You bet. Sometimes it's Cheez-Its from the tackle box and sometimes it's sautéed elk tenderloin (the part the wolves didn't eat while we were retrieving the pack horses) hot from the skillet. Sometimes we've got the Dutch oven oiled for the next batch of cornbread, and sometimes the microwave will have to do. We know how to share. Biscuits during lambing season, Basque stew once the windmill has been repaired, enchiladas delivered to a neighbor's after the birth of a child; Pamela Sinclair reminds us that food is the currency of our culture. It's the jam we slather on sourdough toast at the rodeo breakfast or the pie we slice into portions at a funeral wake. In a state where it snows twelve months of the year, we have learned to bind ourselves together with the salty and the sweet.

Is It Time for Lunch Yet?

People here know how to work up an appetite. Backpackers fantasize about the "real food" they'll eat after a week in the Wind River Mountains living on noodles and trail mix. Roughnecks barrel across basin and range for the nearest prime rib. Nothing tastes better than a cheddar cheese sandwich after hours of fruitless casting along the Platte River, even if there are midges mixed in with the mustard. I've got friends who are, at this moment, lacing up their boots to go mushroom hunting. Morels? In a risotto? In the middle of nowhere? Absolutely. And one of those fool 'shroomers has probably already made the typical 150-mile round trip to the nearest wine store to select just the right vintage of pinot noir.

We're not unsophisticated eaters here; this book is ample evidence of our mixed histories and discerning palates. But our growing season is about the length of a politician's stump speech, so we have become canny and resourceful. Baking, for instance, is a thankless task above 3,000 feet. My own Aunt Lois did me the favor of flying out from Virginia to adjust the clan recipes to the rigors of thin air. I can now approximate a chocolate chess pie well enough to please most church elders. We make do. And when we have the chance, we fill our bellies as if we were Parisians.

Cowboy Java Joe

Before I read (and salivated over) the contents of this book, I would have described Wyoming cuisine as merely anything that goes well with coffee. Boot soles and coffee. Hat brims and coffee. It's impossible to imagine a mythic grizzled wrangler without his ground beans and fire-blackened pot. Thank goodness for Pamela Sinclair and her Ten Sleep Tea. Pamela has rescued me from my own circumscribed myths with these recipes. It's true. I wish she'd saved space for that necessary category of meals that can survive an all-day cross-state high school bus ride. My ravenous teenage son would have been grateful. As it is, he'll have to survive on the Onion Straws and a BLT. Meanwhile, I know you will enjoy the panorama of foodstuffs and photographs contained herein. I surely have. They come from a strange and beautiful place: from my high-flung home of Wyoming, where even the names of towns—Meeteetse, Story, Chugwater, Shell—are tasty with flavor.

Alyson Hagy is the author of five works of fiction. She lives in Laramie and teaches at the University of Wyoming.

acknowledgments

It is with a mountain of gratitude that I recognize everyone who contributed to this unique recipe collection. Thank you to the superb chefs, restaurant proprietors, innkeepers, lodge and ranch owners, general managers, and friendly staff who welcomed me into their charming establishments. All are listed in the appendix, and I encourage you to visit them and indulge in their delicious cuisine served with warm hospitality.

Thank you to Wyoming's governor and first lady, Dave and Nancy Freudenthal, former Wyoming governor Jim Geringer and his wife, Sherri, and Alan K. Simpson, former United States senator from Wyoming, and his wife, Ann, for sharing their favorite family recipes.

Thank you to Alyson Hagy for contributing the foreword and to the distinguished Wyoming writers who share excerpts from their novels, short stories, and poetry. I hope readers will be tempted to venture further into their spirited writing about life in The Cowboy State.

Thank you to Suzi Taylor at the Wyoming State Archives and Betsy Flint at the Jackson Hole Historical Society and Museum for providing exceptional research assistance and historical photographs. My assistant, Samantha Vargas, was a significant source of administrative support, and her attention to detail is commendable.

My family and friends deserve special recognition for embracing this project from the trailhead of my journey to the final destination. I appreciate my husband, John, who was very generous with his assurances and appetite. I am deeply grateful for my lovely mother-in-law, Joyce Sinclair, whose enthusiastic interest in this book nurtured me from start to finish.

I am indebted to Kathy Springmeyer and the staff at Farcountry Press for bringing the book to life. I especially appreciate Jessica Solberg for providing exemplary editorial assistance, along with her guidance, support, and dedication to achieving a unique book. Thank you to Paulette Phlipot for capturing the essence of the chefs' beautiful culinary creations and Wyoming's extraordinary scenery. It is through a collaboration of talent, commitment, and effort that we have created our book.

introduction

"Food is our common ground, a universal experience."

—James Beard, renowned chef and "dean of American cookery"

I have always loved cooking. I remember the first family dinner I prepared when I was about twelve years old. It consisted of meat loaf, mashed potatoes with brown gravy, and fresh green beans from the vegetable garden and became a family favorite. In my childhood Missouri home, the standard culinary fare was meat and potatoes. I had a cooking repertoire limited to variations of those two staples. After college, I was filled with wanderlust and lived in the Caribbean, Chicago, and San Francisco, where I experienced diverse international cuisine. This exposure fed my passion for cooking and insatiable appetite for knowledge about the culinary arts.

After traveling and living in a variety of diverse locations, I chose to settle in my favorite state: Wyoming, where two of my favorite foods, meat and potatoes, reign supreme. The state's long tradition of cattle and sheep ranching and the production of barley, corn, wheat, oats, potatoes, and dry beans shape Wyoming cuisine. Fishing and hunting wild game and fowl are popular activities that also provide abundant fare for the dinner table. Wyoming also holds many delightful culinary surprises you might not expect to find in cowboy country. It is the discovery of these food treasures that has inspired me to create a book that celebrates both Wyoming's rich culinary heritage and its contemporary cuisine. I sought to showcase some of the state's most talented chefs, whose inventive dishes offer a fresh take on the traditional homemade classics, with a few global creations, too.

A Taste of Wyoming is a collection of traditional and gourmet signature recipes from some of Wyoming's most distinctive inns, lodges, guest ranches, resorts, and restaurants. In addition, I have included family favorites from a few of Wyoming's most distinguished residents and some special recipes from my personal collection, which I have developed while living in Wyoming.

Over the years, I have learned that a great-tasting dish combines contrasting flavors that are salty, sour, sweet, and sometimes bitter. It is both an art and a science to achieve a dish that delights the senses of sight, smell, taste, and touch. I have selected a variety of recipes to include in this collection; some are simple and traditional while others are rich and complex. As you venture into this book, you will discover that a number of these recipes reflect Wyoming's diverse ethnic ancestry, including influences from Native Americans, Western frontier people, and European immigrants.

As I traveled across this magnificent state to visit the places where these signature dishes are featured, I was nourished by Wyoming's vast, rugged landscape and towering, majestic mountains—a visual treat that is truly food for the soul. Included in the book are some of these glorious views, captured in beautiful photographs by Paulette Phlipot. I wanted to share a glimpse of Wyoming's spirited past as well, so a few historical photos and vignettes are sprinkled throughout the pages. I also have included excerpts from some of Wyoming's most distinguished writers, who provide lively seasoning with their eloquent words.

It is my hope that you will have as much fun preparing these recipes as I had compiling, testing, and tasting them. Whether you are planning an old-fashioned backyard barbecue, an elegant dinner, a simple family meal, a holiday gathering, or lunch for one, I know you will find the perfect recipe within these pages. Creating this special book for your enjoyment has been a memorable experience. It is a pleasure to share these favorite recipes from The Cowboy State.

guidelines for recipes

Equipment:

    ❧ Oven temperatures are given in degrees Fahrenheit. For best results, always preheat your oven when instructed to do so.

    ❧ Most recipes were developed and tested using professional ranges, so adjustments in cooking and baking time may be necessary. To test baked goods for doneness, insert a clean knife or toothpick into the center of the baked product and remove it gently. If it comes out clean, the product is ready to remove from the oven.

High-Altitude Cooking and Baking:

Air density is higher at sea level, so as elevation increases and air density decreases, cooking and baking are affected in two ways:

    ❧ Water and other liquids boil at lower temperatures and evaporate more quickly. Cooking time is longer as well.

    ❧ Leavening gases in breads and cakes expand more.

Since these recipes were developed and tested at elevations of 3,000 feet or more, the following adjustments may be required when preparing some recipes *below* 3,000 feet (I recommend preparing the dish according to the recipe first, before making any changes):

    ❧ Increase baking powder and baking soda: for each teaspoon listed, increase ⅛ teaspoon.

    ❧ Increase sugar: for each cup of sugar listed, add 1 to 2 tablespoons.

    ❧ Decrease liquid: for each cup of liquid listed, reduce 1 to 2 tablespoons (excluding oils).

    ❧ Lower oven temperature 20 to 25 degrees: note that baking time may need to be adjusted, so watch products closely rather than following recipe directions for cooking/baking times.

Ingredients:

- ❧ *Broth* refers to packaged or canned product, and *stock* refers to homemade.

- ❧ *Butter* refers to unsalted whole butter. For best results, do not use a substitute unless the recipe indicates otherwise.

- ❧ Use canola oil in recipes that require cooking oil and, unless otherwise stated, coat baking dishes and pans with unflavored cooking spray.

- ❧ One tablespoon of fresh herbs is equal to one teaspoon dried.

- ❧ Standard egg size is Large, Grade A.

- ❧ *Sugar* refers to granulated sugar unless stated otherwise.

- ❧ Use a medium-size lemon for recipes calling for lemon juice and zest. A medium-size lemon yields about 2 tablespoons juice and 1 tablespoon zest.

- ❧ A list of sources for specialty ingredients and other products is in the appendix.

Preparation and Servings:

- ❧ *Diced* indicates cutting into ¼- to ½-inch cubes.

- ❧ *Overnight preparation* indicates 8 to 12 hours.

- ❧ Servings listed are approximate and depend on individual preferences for serving amounts.

Utensils:

- ❧ Use a standard meat thermometer to test for desired doneness.

- ❧ A *baking dish* refers to glass and a *baking pan* refers to metal.

- ❧ Standard muffin tins used for recipes are about 2½ inches across the top.

- ❧ A small mixing bowl = about 3 cups, a medium mixing bowl = 6 cups (1½ quarts), and a large mixing bowl = 10 cups (2½ quarts or more).

Breakfast & Brunch

Ten-Grain Pecan Pancakes with Sautéed Apples, p. 16

Blue Ribbon
Caramel Cinnamon Rolls

RED ROCK RANCH, KELLY   PASTRY CHEF ADDIE HARE

Ranch pastry chef Addie Hare won a first-place blue ribbon at the Teton County Fair with her mother's wonderful recipe. Addie writes, "On special Sunday mornings we would awaken to this treat coming out of the oven. We were so spoiled!"

2 cups warm water

2½ teaspoons yeast

1 teaspoon sugar

¼ cup honey

¼ cup vegetable oil

1 tablespoon salt

7 cups all-purpose flour

¼ cup melted butter (½ stick)

Brown sugar for sprinkling

Cinnamon for sprinkling

1 cup heavy cream

Makes 12 rolls

Preheat the oven to 350 degrees. Pour the water into a large mixing bowl and sprinkle the yeast over the water, then sprinkle the sugar over the yeast and water. Allow bubbles to form, about 5 minutes. Stir in the honey, oil, and salt; mix well.

Using an electric mixer with a dough hook, slowly add the flour and mix until the dough does not stick to the sides of the bowl. Place the dough in a separate, lightly oiled bowl to rise until it doubles in size. On a lightly oiled work surface, roll the dough out into a ½-inch-thick rectangle. Brush the melted butter over the dough and sprinkle with brown sugar and cinnamon. Roll the dough loosely into a log shape and pinch the edges to seal.

Cut the dough into 2-inch-thick rolls using a serrated knife. Sprinkle a 13 x 9 x 2-inch baking pan with brown sugar and cinnamon; place the rolls in the pan and cover with a clean towel. Set aside to allow rolls to rise, about 20 to 25 minutes, or cover with plastic wrap and refrigerate until ready to bake.

Sprinkle the tops of the rolls with brown sugar and cinnamon; pour the heavy cream over the rolls and bake for 20 to 25 minutes, until the tops are golden brown. Remove from the oven and invert onto a serving tray or sheet pan.

Blueberry Kuchen

1 cup all-purpose flour

1 ½ teaspoons baking powder

½ teaspoon ground nutmeg

¼ teaspoon salt

¾ cup sugar

½ cup butter at room temperature

2 eggs

1 teaspoon vanilla extract

1 to 2 teaspoons freshly
  grated lemon peel

1 cup fresh or frozen blueberries

Powdered sugar (optional)

Makes 6 to 8 servings

Germans form the largest immigrant group in Wyoming, and kuchen, the German word for cake, is a popular breakfast sweet and dessert. Our neighbors in South Dakota have designated kuchen their state dessert, and North Dakotans call it "kugen." Topped with plump, juicy blueberries, this dense, moist shortcake is a family favorite. For variation, use cherries, raspberries, apricots, peaches, or plums.

Preheat the oven to 350 degrees. In a large mixing bowl, combine the flour, baking powder, nutmeg, and salt; set aside.

In a separate mixing bowl, beat the sugar and butter with an electric mixer until creamy. Beat in the eggs, vanilla extract, and lemon peel; add to the flour mixture and combine well.

Spread the mixture into a lightly oiled, round 9-inch (2 inches deep) baking pan and spread the blueberries evenly over the mixture, pressing them lightly into the batter.

Bake for 35 to 40 minutes, or until lightly browned. Remove from the oven and let rest for 5 minutes before serving. Sprinkle with powdered sugar if desired.

1 ½ cups unbleached flour

⅓ cup sugar

½ cup brown sugar

½ teaspoon ground ginger

½ teaspoon salt

3 teaspoons cinnamon, divided

6 tablespoons softened butter

½ cup chopped pecans

1 egg

⅔ cup buttermilk

½ teaspoon baking soda

½ teaspoon baking powder

Makes 8 servings

Buttermilk Pecan Coffee Cake

THE BUNNERY, JACKSON

For more than three decades, the Bunnery has been a favorite for breakfast and lunch among locals. This is my favorite coffee cake, but I must offer a few words of caution: this delicate cake will fall easily if disturbed during baking, so handle with care.

Preheat the oven to 350 degrees. In a large mixing bowl, combine the flour, sugars, ginger, salt, and 2 teaspoons of the cinnamon. Add the butter and cut into the dry mixture with a fork.

Transfer ⅔ cup of the mixture to a separate bowl. Add the pecans and remaining cinnamon; mix well and set aside for topping.

Beat the egg into the main mixture by hand or with a mixer on low speed. Gradually stir in the buttermilk; whip the batter until it is light and smooth. Add the baking soda and baking powder; mix well.

Spread the batter evenly into a 9-inch ring pan that has been oiled and lined with baking paper. Sprinkle evenly with the reserved pecan crumb mixture.

Bake undisturbed for 25 minutes. Let the cake rest for 5 minutes before removing from the pan.

Cowboy Cheese Grits

THE HOWDY PARDNER BED AND BREAKFAST, CHEYENNE

2 eggs

3 cups water

1 teaspoon salt

¾ cup uncooked grits

6 tablespoons butter or margarine

½ pound processed cheese,
    cut into 1-inch chunks

¼ teaspoon red pepper (optional)

Makes 8 to 10 servings

Grits are made from hominy or plain corn that has been ground to the consistency of coarse sand. Grits are most often used as a breakfast cereal, a side dish, or as an ingredient in baked goods. These creamy breakfast grits are baked and may be prepared a day ahead.

Preheat the oven to 350 degrees. Whisk the eggs in a small bowl and set aside. In a medium saucepan, bring the water and salt to a boil; add the grits slowly, stirring constantly. Cook over medium heat until thick, about 5 minutes.

Lower the heat to simmer and stir in the butter or margarine, cheese, and pepper. Stir in the eggs and cook until the cheese is melted.

Transfer the mixture to a baking dish coated with cooking spray and bake for 40 to 45 minutes.

PUBLISHED IN *HOT BISCUITS: EIGHTEEN STORIES BY WOMEN AND MEN OF THE RANCHING WEST* BY THE UNIVERSITY OF MEXICO PRESS IN 2002

FROM "NATURAL CAUSES"
BY LORI VAN PELT

Anna said, "Do you want cream on your dessert, Carl?"

Carl shook his head. "No, thanks. Cream's too heavy for me today."

She smiled at him and dished up the apple crisp. Handing him his portion, she said, "I warmed it in the oven while we were eating."

He took a bite, letting the cinnamon caress his nose and savoring the soft warm apple slices and brown sugar's crunchier texture. The sweetness soothed him. He said, "Mm, Anna, this is good crisp."

She thanked him, said, "Better than bride's crisp?" They both laughed at the joke he'd made when they'd been newly married ten years before. Carl's way of complimenting her cooking was to tell her the meal was "better than bride's cooking." He'd complimented her often for her tasty cooking since, expecially her homemade biscuits. He never tired of eating them. Sometimes for breakfast, she'd fry up some ham and make gravy to go with them. He savored the taste of those light biscuits doused with thick, creamy ham gravy. For morning snacks, he usually covered a biscuit or two with a good helping of salty butter and a healthy dollop of Anna's sweet chokecherry jelly. A fresh, warm pan of Anna's golden, airy biscuits gave a man the strength to go on, especially when things looked bad.

Barthy Moulton makes butter in her kitchen on Mormon Row.
COURTESY PHIL SULTZ, COLLECTION OF THE JACKSON HOLE HISTORICAL SOCIETY AND MUSEUM, 2004.0048.001

3 cups all-purpose flour

⅓ cup sugar

2½ teaspoons baking powder

½ teaspoon baking soda

¾ teaspoon salt

¾ cup firm butter, cut into
small pieces

¾ cup chopped fresh or
dried cranberries

1 teaspoon freshly
grated orange zest

1 cup buttermilk

Cinnamon to taste

Sugar to taste

Makes 12 scones

Cranberry-Orange Scones

THE WILDFLOWER INN, JACKSON HOLE

Filled with tangy, nutritious cranberries and fragrant orange zest, this is a light, flaky, biscuitlike scone that may simply be described as scrumptious!

Preheat the oven to 425 degrees. In a large mixing bowl, combine the flour, sugar, baking powder, baking soda, and salt.

Cut the butter into the mixture with a fork until the dough resembles coarse crumbs.

Mix in the cranberries and orange zest. Add the buttermilk and stir until a dough ball can be formed (use a light hand for flaky scones).

Divide the dough into 2 equal balls; roll out each dough ball on a floured surface to ¾-inch thickness. Cut each flattened dough circle into 6 equal wedges or use a heart-shaped cookie cutter (during the Christmas holiday, I use a star-shaped cookie cutter).

Place the cut dough on a baking sheet lined with parchment paper, sprinkle with cinnamon and sugar, and bake for 12 minutes or until brown.

3 eggs

1 ¼ cups whole or reduced-fat milk

3 tablespoons canola oil, divided

½ cup all-purpose flour

¼ cup whole-wheat flour

½ teaspoon salt

1 teaspoon sugar (optional)

Makes 2 to 3 servings

Wyoming is listed in the top ten states in number of Swedish descendants.

Dad's Sweetie Pancakes

FORMER WYOMING GOVERNOR JIM GERINGER, WHEATLAND

Geringer began preparing this delicious dish after discovering the recipe hanging on a wall at the home of a fellow church member, who later presented the recipe as a gift, along with a plattpan. A plattpan is a skillet that has several round indentations into which pancake batter is poured and cooked. This delicious recipe is now a Geringer family favorite and acquired its unique name from one of the Geringers' grandsons, who has his own unique pronunciation of "Swedish." Geringer, whose mother's family were Swedish immigrants, wrote, "Mom encouraged each of her seven children to take a turn in the kitchen, an experience I'll always treasure." Traditionally served with lingonberry jam and powdered sugar, other toppings include butter, honey, or your favorite berry jam. Simply double the recipe for more servings.

Beat the eggs in a mixing bowl until they are light and fluffy. Stir in the milk and 2 tablespoons of the oil.

In a separate large mixing bowl, combine the all-purpose and whole-wheat flour and salt—and the sugar, if desired. Whisk the liquid mixture into the dry mixture; it should be thin.

Lightly oil the plattpan or a 6-inch cast-iron skillet with the remaining oil and set the pan over medium heat for about 30 seconds. To test if the pan is hot enough, drop a tiny bit of water in the pan; when it sizzles, the pan is ready. Pour the batter into the plattpan or skillet, using only enough batter to fill the space. Cook the pancakes until lightly browned, about 1 to 2 minutes on each side. Remove from the pan and repeat the process. Keep the cooked pancakes warm in the oven at 200 degrees until ready to serve.

4 slices thick-cut bacon
(or 1 slice of ham or
2 pork sausage patties)

2 eggs

2 slices American cheese

2 large slices sourdough bread

1 to 2 tablespoons butter

2 thin slices red onion

2 slices fresh tomato

Makes 1 sandwich

Moosey Breakfast Sam'wich

WALDORF A'STORY AT PINEY CREEK GENERAL STORE, STORY

How this "sam'wich" acquired its unique name is a mystery, but this is a favorite on the menu at the cozy restaurant in Story, a tiny hamlet tucked into the base of the Big Horn Mountains. The breakfast sandwich is offered with one of three meat choices: bacon, ham, or pork sausage patties. I prepare it with bacon and serve with roasted new potatoes.

Cook the bacon or other meat over medium heat in a large skillet. Remove and place on a paper towel to allow the oil to drain; set aside.

Add the eggs to the skillet and cook over low heat, scrambling them slightly. Place the sliced cheese on top of the eggs and cover for 2 to 3 minutes, until the cheese is melted.

Butter one side of each piece of bread and lay both slices, buttered side down, on a preheated griddle or in a fry pan; cook over low heat until golden brown.

Set the eggs and cheese on the unbuttered side of a slice of bread, add the meat, and place the sliced onion and tomato over the eggs and cheese; cover with the other slice of bread, buttered side up, and cut the sandwich in half. Serve immediately.

2 firm, ripe pears, peeled
   and cut into ½-inch chunks

2 tablespoons butter or margarine

6 eggs

⅓ cup milk

¼ cup all-purpose flour

1 tablespoon sugar

1 teaspoon vanilla extract

¼ teaspoon salt

¼ cup whipped cream cheese

2 tablespoons brown sugar

Makes 6 to 8 servings

Pear Frittata

DEVILS TOWER LODGE, DEVILS TOWER

Pears add a buttery texture and subtle sweetness to this baked egg dish. An excellent choice for a brunch buffet, this dish also may be served as a dessert.

Preheat the oven to 425 degrees. Melt the butter or margarine in a nonstick skillet over medium-low heat and sauté the pears until lightly browned. Transfer to a lightly buttered 9-inch round baking dish.

In a large mixing bowl, whisk the eggs, milk, flour, sugar, vanilla extract, and salt. Pour the egg mixture over the pears and bake for 10 to 12 minutes.

Remove from the oven and let rest for 5 minutes before cutting into wedges. Spoon desired amount of whipped cream cheese over each serving portion and sprinkle with brown sugar to taste.

French toast

4 eggs

1 cup heavy cream

1 tablespoon maple syrup

½ teaspoon vanilla extract

1 tablespoon Grand Marnier liqueur

1 teaspoon ground cinnamon,
  divided

⅛ teaspoon ground nutmeg

6 (½-inch thick) slices brioche bread,
  cut into halves

3 tablespoons butter

Ricotta cheese

1 quart whole milk

2 tablespoons fresh lemon juice

Makes 6 servings

Stuffed Brioche French Toast with Peach, Pecan, and Vanilla Honey Syrup

THE ALPINE HOUSE, JACKSON   ❧   CHEF JEFFREY FRANKLIN

The perfect bread for making French toast, brioche is a light and fluffy egg bread that absorbs the batter very well. The chef recommends cooking the sliced bread over low heat to maintain moistness. Although the chef makes his own ricotta cheese, you may substitute prepared ricotta if desired.

To prepare the French toast:
In a large mixing bowl, whisk together the eggs, cream, maple syrup, vanilla extract, liqueur, ¼ teaspoon cinnamon, and nutmeg. Pour the egg mixture into a 13 x 9 x 2-inch baking dish and place the sliced bread in the dish. Turn the bread slices several times to absorb the mixture.

Heat the butter over medium–low heat in a large nonstick skillet or griddle. When the butter begins to bubble, place the bread slices in the pan and cook for 5 to 6 minutes on each side, or until golden brown.

To prepare the ricotta cheese:
Heat the milk in a heavy saucepan over medium heat, being careful not to scald. Stir in the lemon juice and cook over medium heat to 200 degrees (test the heat with a candy thermometer). Remove the pan from the heat and cover; set aside to rest undisturbed for 15 minutes. Line a colander with fine cheesecloth and slowly pour the milk into the colander. Set aside to drain for 1 hour.

(continued page 14)

Peach, pecan, and vanilla honey syrup

1 cup honey

4 ripe white peaches, pitted and cut into eighths

1 teaspoon vanilla extract

⅓ cup coarsely chopped toasted pecans

¼ cup Grand Marnier liqueur

Makes 6 servings

To prepare the peach, pecan, and vanilla honey syrup:
Heat the honey over low heat in a medium saucepan, about 5 minutes. Add the peaches, vanilla, pecans, and liqueur and simmer for 10 minutes, or until warmed through.

Presentation:
Place the sliced toast on a plate and top with 2 tablespoons of warm ricotta cheese. Place another slice of toast over the cheese and drizzle with warm honey syrup. Sprinkle a light dusting of ground cinnamon on the plate around the French toast and serve immediately.

2 cups crumbled cooked sausage

½ cup sliced green onions

½ cup finely chopped
    green bell pepper

2½ cups shredded cheddar
    cheese, divided

8 whole green roasted chiles,
    stems and seeds removed

8 (7-inch) flour tortillas

4 eggs

2 cups light cream

1 tablespoon all-purpose flour

¼ teaspoon salt

1 to 2 garlic cloves, minced

Hot pepper sauce (optional)

Optional garnishes

Avocado slices

Cilantro, freshly chopped

Salsa

Sour cream

Makes 6 to 8 servings

Sunrise Enchiladas

PORCH SWING BED AND BREAKFAST, CHEYENNE

A guest favorite at this quaint bed and breakfast, this signature egg dish can be prepared a day ahead. Substitute the sausage with crumbled bacon or chopped ham for tasty variations.

Preheat the oven to 350 degrees. In a mixing bowl, combine the cooked sausage, onions, bell pepper, and ⅓ cup plus 3 tablespoons of the cheese.

Create a lengthwise slit in each chile and open. Place a flattened chile on one end of a tortilla and spoon about ¼ cup of the sausage mixture over the chile. Roll the tortilla and place it seam side down in a lightly oiled 13 x 9 x 2-inch baking dish. Repeat for the remaining tortillas.

In a separate mixing bowl, combine the eggs, cream, flour, salt, garlic, and hot sauce and pour the mixture over the prepared tortillas. If making this dish a day ahead, cover the baking dish with plastic wrap and refrigerate overnight.

Bake for 45 to 50 minutes. Remove from the oven, cover with the remaining cheese, and return to the oven. Bake 3 to 5 more minutes, or until the cheese has melted.

Pancakes

½ cup 10-grain flour

½ cup cake flour

½ teaspoon baking powder

½ teaspoon baking soda

¼ teaspoon salt

1 egg

1 tablespoon canola oil

1 cup milk

1 teaspoon vanilla extract

Powdered sugar (optional)

1 cup whipped cream

1 cup toasted whole pecans

Sautéed apples

2 apples, cored, peeled, and
    cut into ½-inch cubes

1 tablespoon butter

2 tablespoons sugar

½ teaspoon cinnamon

Makes 4 to 6 servings

For a tender, aromatic apple, select
Jonagold, Fuji, Gala, or Pink Lady;
if you prefer a more crisp–tender
variety, choose Red Delicious,
Granny Smith, or Macintosh.

Ten-Grain Pecan Pancakes with Sautéed Apples

GRAND VICTORIAN LODGE, JACKSON
OWNER/CHEF THOMAS STODOLA

Start an active day with this delicious, healthy breakfast! The key ingredient for making these wholesome, nutritious pancakes is the ten-grain flour. Multi-grain or whole grain flour may also be used.

To prepare the pancakes:
Sift the flours, baking powder, baking soda, and salt together in a large mixing bowl.

In a separate mixing bowl, whisk the egg, oil, milk, and vanilla extract; stir into the flour mixture until a smooth batter forms.

Heat a large fry pan or griddle over medium heat; for each pancake, pour 4 tablespoons of batter into the pan or griddle. Bubbles should form within 1 minute and edges should appear dry; flip pancakes and cook for about 1 minute, or until cooked through. Remove from the pan and sprinkle lightly with powdered sugar.

To prepare the sautéed apples:
Melt the butter in a saucepan over low heat, add the apples, and cover. Cook over low heat until tender, about 10 minutes. Add the sugar and cinnamon; increase the heat to medium–high and stir until bubbly. Remove from the heat and serve over the pancakes or on the side.

Presentation:
Top each serving with a dollop of whipped cream and sprinkle with toasted pecans.

(See photograph on page 1)

Pie shell

1 cup all-purpose flour

1 teaspoon salt

1 ½ teaspoons chili powder

1 ½ teaspoons sugar

⅓ cup shortening

¼ cup ice water

½ teaspoon white vinegar

Filling

¾ cup grated cheddar cheese

½ cup grated
  Monterey Jack cheese

3 eggs, lightly beaten

1 teaspoon salt

¼ teaspoon white pepper

1 ½ cups half-and-half

½ cup chopped green chiles

¼ cup sliced ripe olives

2 tablespoons finely
  chopped green onions

Makes 1 (9-inch) pie

Western Quiche

FLYING A RANCH, PINEDALE

Add cooked crumbled sausage or bacon or sliced Canadian bacon to this popular breakfast pie for variety. Note the pie shell recipe is included; it is an important part of this recipe because it contains chili powder, giving this traditional quiche its Western flair. To save time, purchase a frozen unbaked pie shell and sprinkle with a pinch of chili powder before adding the filling.

To prepare the pie shell:
In a large mixing bowl, combine the flour, salt, chili powder, and sugar; cut in the shortening until the mixture is crumbly.

In a small mixing bowl, combine the ice water and the vinegar; slowly pour it over the flour mixture, 1 tablespoon at a time, stirring with a fork until the flour mixture is moistened and can be formed into a ball. Avoid adding too much water or over-mixing.

Place the ball of dough on a lightly floured surface and flatten it with your hand. Roll out the dough until it fits a 9-inch pie dish. Lightly oil the pie dish, fold the dough into thirds, and transfer it to the pie dish. Unfold and pat it gently into the dish, being careful not to stretch or tear the pastry. After trimming the edges, flute them with your thumb and forefinger.

Cover loosely with plastic wrap and refrigerate for 15 minutes. Prick the dough with a fork two to three times and pour the filling into the pie shell.

To prepare the filling:
Preheat the oven to 350 degrees. Combine the grated cheeses in a mixing bowl and spread over the bottom of the prepared pie shell. In a large mixing bowl, combine the eggs, salt, pepper, half-and-half, chiles, olives, and onions. Pour over the cheese and bake for 40 to 45 minutes.

8 to 10 cups old-fashioned
    Quaker Oats

2 cups shredded coconut

1 cup assorted unsalted nuts
    and seeds (sliced almonds,
    walnuts, pecans, sunflower
    seeds, pumpkin seeds)

1 cup melted butter (2 sticks)

1 cup honey

2 cups mixed dried fruit
    (raisins, cranberries, apples,
    apricots, bananas, dates)

Makes 10 to 15 cups

Wildflower Inn Granola

THE WILDFLOWER INN, JACKSON HOLE

Top this healthy breakfast cereal with a dollop of creamy vanilla yogurt and a light sprinkling of cinnamon. In the summer, I omit the dried fruit and sprinkle with fresh berries. For an attractive presentation, layer the granola with yogurt and fresh fruit in parfait glasses.

Preheat the oven to 350 degrees. Mix the oats, coconut, nuts, and seeds in a large roasting pan.

Melt the butter and honey in a saucepan over low heat or in the microwave and combine with the oat mixture.

Roast the oat mixture in the oven until golden brown, about 30 to 45 minutes. Stir the mixture well every 15 minutes and watch it carefully to avoid burning.

Remove the oat mixture from the oven, cool, and stir in the fruit. Store in an airtight container.

Appetizers & Snacks

Pine Nut–Crusted Goat Cheese, p. 32

½ cup dried apples

¼ cup raisins

¼ cup dried cranberries

1 cup yogurt-coated mini pretzels

1 cup salted sunflower seeds

1 cup salted mixed nuts
(almonds, cashews, walnuts,
peanuts)

Makes 4 cups

Alpine Trail Mix

A perfect snack on an active day, this blend of sweet and salty flavors is a healthy and delicious way to replenish energy. Any combination of your favorite dried fruits and nuts may be substituted to suit your taste. Add honey-roasted nuts or a few chocolate chips if you like more sweet nuggets.

Combine all of the ingredients in a large mixing bowl and store in an airtight container for up to 2 weeks.

4 cups all-purpose flour

1 tablespoon baking powder

½ teaspoon salt

1½ to 1¾ cups warm water

¼ cup canola oil

Makes 8 (4-inch) pieces

American Indian Fry Bread

Fry bread evolved in the 1800s when the U.S. government forced American Indian tribes onto reservations. The government provided them with provisions of flour and lard, and this flat bread became a staple of their diet. This simple bread is excellent for making tacos or served with soup, stew, or chili. It may also be served as a sweet treat topped with honey, chokecherry jam, fresh berries, or cinnamon and sugar. Cook in a well-seasoned cast-iron skillet for tastier fry bread.

Combine the flour, baking powder, and salt in a large mixing bowl; slowly add the water, stirring until the dough becomes soft (avoid over-mixing so the dough does not become sticky). Cover with plastic wrap and set aside to rest for 30 minutes.

Form the dough into balls, each about the size of a large lemon, and flatten them into round patties about ¼-inch thick. Punch a small hole in the center of each piece so the dough will cook more evenly and not burst.

Heat the oil in a heavy cast-iron skillet over medium-high heat and cook the flattened dough patties about 2 to 3 minutes on each side until lightly browned and cooked through. Add more oil as needed. Drain on absorbent paper and serve.

The chokecherry, a member of the plum family, is common in the eastern and western United States and most of Canada. Able to tolerate both drought conditions and harsh winters, the chokecherry was an important part of the Native Americans' diet. After harvesting the berries, they stored them for winter in a partly dried or frozen state; the berries served as a valuable source of food during the long winter season. The chokecherries were mixed with fat and suet, then pounded into buffalo meat. This mixture of meat, fruit, and fat is known as pemmican and was a staple of the prairie tribes. Although some native people still make pemmican, today chokecherries are more frequently used to make wine, syrup, jelly, and jam.

1 cup sour cream

1 cup cream cheese, softened

¾ cup Asiago cheese

2 tablespoons Pecorino
    Romano cheese

¾ cup coarsely chopped
    artichoke hearts

¼ cup finely chopped sun-dried
    tomatoes (reserve 1 tablespoon
    for garnish)

½ teaspoon granulated garlic

½ teaspoon red pepper flakes

Salt to taste

Makes 4 cups

Asiago Cheese Dip

SHADOWS BREWING COMPANY, CHEYENNE

Asiago, pronounced AH–see–AH–go, is a European cheese with a distinct, nutty flavor. It is known as a "mountain cheese" because it is produced using milk from cows that graze on lush mountain pastures. The sun-dried tomatoes and artichoke hearts add rich flavor and texture to this creamy dip. Spread on thick slices of warmed baguettes or focaccia, an Italian flat bread used for sandwiches.

Combine the sour cream, cream cheese, Asiago and Pecorino Romano cheeses, artichoke hearts, sun-dried tomatoes, garlic, and pepper flakes in a mixing bowl and heat the mixture in a microwave oven or fondue pot until warmed through. Garnish with the remaining chopped sun-dried tomato and serve immediately.

Jam

2 cups fresh or frozen lingonberries

Dash water (or more as needed)

½ to ¾ cup sugar

1 tablespoon unflavored gelatin
(or ¼-ounce envelope)

Candied walnuts

2 cups raw walnut halves

½ cup brown sugar

2 to 3 teaspoons almond extract

1 tablespoon water

Baked Brie in baguettes

2 large loaves of fresh
French baguettes

12 to 16 ounces Brie cheese

Makes 12 servings

Baked Brie in Baguettes with Lingonberry Jam and Candied Walnuts

THE GRANARY RESTAURANT AT SPRING CREEK RANCH, JACKSON
EXECUTIVE CHEF JASON MITCHELL

Lingonberries are similar to cranberries but smaller and not as tangy. You can find lingonberry jam at specialty stores or substitute with cranberry jam. Prepare the candied walnuts and jam prior to baking the baguettes.

To prepare the jam:
In a 2-quart saucepan, combine the berries, water, and sugar; cook over high heat to bring to a low boil, then lower the heat to simmer. Add the gelatin and stir frequently until the gelatin dissolves. Remove from the heat and set aside to cool until ready to serve.

To prepare the candied walnuts:
Heat a large skillet over medium heat and add the walnuts. Toast the walnuts while stirring constantly for 1 to 2 minutes; add the brown sugar and almond extract while continuing to stir for 1 to 2 minutes. Add the water, stir another 1 minute, and remove from the heat. Let cool until ready to serve.

To prepare the baked Brie in baguettes:
Preheat the oven to 400 degrees. Slice off the ends of the baguettes, then slice the two baguettes into thirds so you have six (6-inch-long) demi-baguettes. Remove the bread from the center of each baguette to create bread tubes (about 3 inches in diamter) with a 1-inch opening.

(continued page 24)

The lingonberry, also known as the dry ground cranberry, is a wild fruit species commonly found in the mountainous regions of Scandinavia, Russia, Canada, and the United States. Historical documentation suggests that many European explorers and native people considered lingonberry to be a highly valuable fruit. Although frequently compared to the cranberry, the lingonberry has a distinct, uniquely intense flavor unlike any other.

Remove the rind from the Brie and cut it into 1-inch cubes; fill the bread tubes with the cut Brie.

Using a serrated knife, cut "semi-slices" (don't slice through) in the baguettes ½-inch apart.

Transfer the baguettes to a baking sheet and bake for 10 minutes, or until golden and the Brie has melted.

Presentation:
Place the loaves on a serving platter(s) with a large dollop of jam on the side and candied walnuts around the baguettes.

PUBLISHED BY SKINNER HOUSE BOOKS IN 2004

FROM PRAIRIE SOUL: FINDING GRACE IN THE EARTH BENEATH MY FEET
BY JEFFREY A. LOCKWOOD

Grass unites humankind. In the most fundamental sense, the staple foods of the world are based on grasses. Humans may be divided by politics, but we're united at the dinner table. The annual global harvest of just four grasses—sugarcane, corn, rice, wheat—is greater than the total production of all 128 other food crops grown on earth. These four grasses are harvested from two million square miles of the earth's surface. That's like planting a field extending from Canada to Mexico and from the Mississippi to the Pacific. Although we've converted much of the grassland biome into the breadbasket of humanity, nearly a quarter of the land is still blanketed by native grasses in places that are too dry and cold to plow—like most of Wyoming and Kazakhstan.

4 grilled boneless, skinless
chicken breasts

¼ cup red hot pepper sauce

6 large chipotle tortillas

¾ cup Gorgonzola
cheese dressing

1 ½ cups coarsely chopped
fresh spinach

¾ cups shredded pepper
Jack cheese

Makes 4 to 6 servings

Buffalo Chicken Wraps

LOVEJOY'S BAR AND GRILL, LARAMIE

This signature appetizer features a distinctive combination of flavors and a spicy kick. For a milder flavor, substitute mild pepper sauce and use Monterey Jack cheese.

Preheat the oven to 350 degrees. Dice the chicken breasts into ½-inch cubes and lightly toss with the hot pepper sauce in a large mixing bowl until the chicken is coated.

Spread an even amount of the diced chicken in the center of each tortilla. Add the Gorgonzola dressing, fresh spinach, and pepper Jack cheese to each tortilla.

Roll the tortillas tightly and bake for 10 to 15 minutes, or until warmed through and the cheese is melted. Slice the tortillas on the diagonal into halves or thirds and serve them warm on a platter with dressing on the side.

Crab cakes

1 egg

4 tablespoons mayonnaise

2 tablespoons melted butter

Juice and zest of 1 lemon

1 teaspoon Cajun seasoning

10 to 12 finely crushed
    saltine crackers

1 to 1 1/4 pounds fresh, cleaned,
    and drained crab meat

2 tablespoons olive oil

Dipping sauce

1 roasted chipotle pepper,
    finely chopped

1 (7-ounce) jar Asian plum sauce

1 plum, peeled and finely chopped

Makes about 12 to 15 cakes

Crab Cakes with Chipotle-Plum Dipping Sauce

RANGER CREEK GUEST RANCH, SHELL
CHEF AMANDA SCHROEDER

These superb appetizers disappear quickly, so you may want to double the recipe. In addition to serving as appetizers, I have prepared these for dinner by simply making the cakes larger and presenting them with a mixed green salad.

To prepare the crab cakes:
Combine the egg, mayonnaise, butter, lemon juice and zest, seasoning, and crackers in a large mixing bowl; gently stir in the crab meat with a spatula and mix well.

Fill a 1/4-cup measuring cup to form the mixture into cakes; place them onto a large plate. Refrigerate for 30 minutes, or until ready to prepare.

Heat the oil in a large nonstick skillet over medium heat; cook the cakes in batches for about 4 minutes on each side, turning once, until golden brown (add more olive oil as needed). Drain them on paper towels and serve with warm dipping sauce.

To prepare the dipping sauce:
Combine the chopped chipotle pepper, plum sauce, and chopped plum in a small saucepan and warm over low heat until ready to serve.

1 cup buttermilk

2 white onions, peeled
and thinly sliced

1 cup all-purpose flour

1 ½ teaspoons paprika

1 ½ teaspoons powdered garlic

1 teaspoon salt

½ teaspoon black pepper

½ to 1 cup canola oil

Makes 4 to 6 servings

Onion Straws

FIRE ROCK STEAKHOUSE AND GRILL, CASPER
CHEFS JEREMY MIDDLETON AND VICKY EASTON

*Serve these crispy onions with ketchup or with your favorite dipping sauce.
The chefs at the restaurant serve these as a side with their signature meat
loaf (see the Fire Rock Meat Loaf recipe in the Main Courses section).*

Pour the buttermilk into a medium–size mixing bowl. Separate the
onion slices and add them to the buttermilk.

In a separate mixing bowl, combine the flour, paprika, garlic, salt,
and pepper.

Strain the buttermilk from the onion slices and coat the separated
onion pieces with the flour mixture; shake off the excess flour.

Heat the oil in a deep fryer or large skillet to 375 degrees. Cook the
onions in small batches until golden brown and crispy (add more oil
as needed). Remove them from the pan and drain on paper towels.

Sign on Teton Pass near Jackson Hole.
COLLECTION OF THE JACKSON
HOLE HISTORICAL SOCIETY AND
MUSEUM, 1958.1206.001

1 cup balsamic vinegar

8 ounces thinly sliced pancetta

1 pound chicken livers,
     cut into halves

2 tablespoons butter

10 to 12 thin onion slices

Brioche (or other rich egg bread)

6 to 8 ounces micro-greens

Makes 4 to 6 servings

Named after trapper and trader David Edward Jackson, Jackson Hole and Jackson are two distinct areas. Jackson Hole refers to the valley in west-central Wyoming; fur trappers referred to it as such because when they entered the valley over the steep slopes, it felt as though they were descending into a hole. The town of Jackson is located at the southern end of the valley.

Pancetta-Wrapped Chicken Livers

JENNY LAKE LODGE, JACKSON HOLE
EXECUTIVE CHEF JOSHUA CONRAD

I had the opportunity to enjoy this splendid appetizer while staying at Jenny Lake Lodge one summer. Micro-greens are the early sprout growth of greens or herbs that are less than fourteen days old; they are intensely flavorful. You may substitute arugula for the micro-greens if necessary.

Heat the balsamic vinegar in a small saucepan over high heat and boil until reduced to about ¼ cup of syrup. Remove from the heat and set aside.

Cut the pancetta into strips wide enough to wrap around the chicken liver pieces. Wrap a single strip of pancetta around each chicken liver and secure it with appetizer picks if necessary.

In a large skillet, melt the butter over medium-high heat and sear the liver pieces on both sides, turning only once. Remove from the heat and set aside until ready to assemble.

Add the sliced onions and more butter if needed; cover and cook over medium-low heat, stirring occasionally until the onions are softened, about 10 minutes. Uncover and continue to cook the onions until they are a rich, dark brown color, about 20 to 25 more minutes.

Presentation:
Place thin slices of brioche on a serving platter, thinly layer with onions and micro-greens, and top with wrapped chicken livers. Drizzle the balsamic vinegar syrup over the livers to finish.

1 tablespoon canola oil

¼ cup shredded Parmesan
    cheese

2 slices sourdough bread

2 slices Monterey Jack cheese

4 slices smoked turkey breast

1 tablespoon chopped red onion

1 tablespoon chopped
    green bell pepper

¼ cup Thousand Island
    salad dressing

Makes 1 sandwich

Parmesan-Crusted Turkey Sandwich

YELLOWSTONE NATIONAL PARK
EXECUTIVE SOUS CHEF MIKE DEAN

Your family and guests will feel like they are dining in a fine restaurant when served this unique sandwich!

Lightly oil a nonstick pan or griddle and heat over low heat. Sprinkle the shredded Parmesan directly into the pan or griddle, covering an area equal in size to the two bread slices placed side by side.

Place the bread into the pan. Place the two slices of Monterey Jack cheese on one slice of bread, and place the turkey slices on the other slice of bread.

Sprinkle the onion and green pepper evenly over the turkey, top with the dressing, then place the bread slice with Monterey Jack cheese on top. Continue cooking over low heat until the cheese is melted and the sandwich is warmed through. Cut in half and serve.

"In 1881 I went to Wyoming and returned in 1882 to Miles city and took up a ranch on the Yellow Stone, raising stock and cattle; also kept a way side inn, where the weary traveler could be accommodated with food, drink, or trouble if he looked for it."
—Calamity Jane, in her autobiography titled *The Life and Adventures of Calamity Jane*

1 pound log goat cheese (chèvre)

½ cup pine nuts

½ cup bread crumbs

½ cup all-purpose flour

Salt and white pepper to taste

2 eggs

2 tablespoons plus 2 teaspoons
    extra-virgin olive oil, divided

¾ cup baby arugula

½ cup strawberry marmalade
    (optional)

Makes 8 servings

Pine Nut–Crusted Goat Cheese

GAMEFISH RESTAURANT AT SNAKE RIVER LODGE AND SPA,
JACKSON HOLE   ❧   EXECUTIVE CHEF KEVIN HUMPHREYS

Goat cheese has a tart flavor that easily distinguishes it from other cheeses. There are a variety of goat cheeses available in most markets, and if you choose to substitute the French-style chèvre, select a soft, fresh variety.

Slice the goat cheese into eight (2-ounce) patties. Cover with plastic wrap and refrigerate.

In a food processor, pulse the pine nuts and bread crumbs until fine; set aside on a plate.

In a small mixing bowl, combine the flour, salt, and white pepper.

In a separate bowl, beat the eggs.

Remove the goat cheese patties from the refrigerator and dredge one patty at a time in the flour mixture.

Toss each floured goat cheese patty in the egg mixture; when coated with egg, transfer the goat cheese to the pine nut/bread crumb mixture and pack the mixture evenly around each patty. Place the coated patties on a plate, cover them with plastic wrap, and refrigerate them until chilled.

Heat 2 tablespoons of olive oil in a skillet over medium-high heat and place the patties in the hot oil. Cook, turning once, until both sides of the patties develop a golden brown crust, about 10 minutes. (Caution: avoid overcooking because the patties will explode if cooked too hot.) Remove the patties from the pan and drain them on paper towels.

Presentation:
Toss the arugula with 2 teaspoons of olive oil and a pinch of salt in a small bowl. Arrange a small amount of arugula on each plate and place a goat cheese patty on top. Spoon a tablespoon of strawberry marmalade on the side.

(See photograph on page 19)

8 ounces cream cheese

¼ cup heavy cream

1 teaspoon fresh lemon juice

Dash hot sauce

8 ounces smoked salmon

2 tablespoons finely chopped
   chives (optional)

Makes 2 cups

Smoked Salmon Spread

For a simple appetizer, prepare this ahead of time and take it out of the refrigerator half an hour before serving. Spread it on gourmet crackers or thinly sliced baguettes.

Combine the cream cheese, cream, lemon juice, and hot sauce in a mixing bowl. Stir in the salmon and mix until creamy and smooth. Sprinkle with the chopped chives and serve.

Formal Wyoming picnic in the badlands. WYOMING STATE ARCHIVES, DEPARTMENT OF STATE PARKS AND CULTURAL RESOURCES, WACKER NEG 95

Toasted crostini

1 large garlic bulb

1 tablespoon olive oil

12 (⅓-inch) slices French bread

Mushroom sauce

1 tablespoon olive oil

40 crimini mushrooms

Salt and freshly ground
　　black pepper to taste

4 tablespoons amaretto liqueur
　　(or 2 tablespoons almond
　　extract)

½ cup heavy cream

¼ teaspoon freshly grated nutmeg

Mixed greens

1 cup spring mix lettuce

2 tablespoons extra-virgin olive oil

1 tablespoon apple cider vinegar

¼ cup freshly grated
　　Parmesan cheese

1 green onion, thinly sliced

Makes 4 servings

Toasted Crostini with Crimini Mushroom Sauce on Mixed Greens

RANGER CREEK GUEST RANCH, SHELL
CHEF AMANDA SCHROEDER

Impress your dinner guests with this sophisticated restaurant-style appetizer that is a perfect accompaniment to a simple baked chicken and rice entrée. You may substitute the amaretto, an almond-flavored Italian liqueur, with almond extract.

To prepare the toasted crostini:
Preheat the oven to 350 degrees. Drizzle the garlic bulb with olive oil and roast it in the oven for 30 minutes, or until the garlic has softened. Remove it from the oven, cut off the top third of the bulb, and squeeze the roasted garlic into a bowl. Mash the garlic with a fork into a smooth paste and set aside.

Place the bread slices on a large baking sheet and bake them for 3 minutes on each side, or until the bread is lightly toasted. Remove the slices from the oven and spread ½ teaspoon of the roasted garlic paste on each crostini. Set aside.

To prepare the mushroom sauce:
Heat the olive oil in a large skillet over medium heat and add the mushrooms. Sauté until the mushrooms just begin to soften.

Add the salt, pepper, and amaretto (or almond extract); stir over medium heat for 2 to 3 minutes to deglaze the pan; add the cream and nutmeg and heat through another 1 to 2 minutes.

To prepare mixed greens:
Whisk the olive oil and vinegar in a mixing bowl; add the greens and toss gently to coat.

Presentation:
Place a small amount of the greens in the center of four plates and arrange three crostini around the greens. Top each crostini with a small amount of mushroom sauce, then sprinkle with grated Parmesan and sliced green onions.

Salads & Sides

Governor's Spinach and Strawberry Salad, p. 39

1 cup vegetable oil

1 cup white vinegar

1 cup sugar

1 teaspoon salt

1 teaspoon dry mustard

1 teaspoon celery seeds

2 cups shredded red cabbage

2 cups shredded green cabbage

1 cup thinly sliced red onion

1 cup grated carrots

1 cup sliced celery

½ cup thinly sliced green pepper

Makes 10 servings

Colorful Cabbage Salad

FLYING A RANCH, PINEDALE

Prepare this vibrant salad the day before a gathering and serve with your favorite grilled or barbecued entrée.

Combine the oil, vinegar, sugar, salt, dry mustard, and celery seeds in a medium saucepan. Cook over medium heat until the sugar dissolves, stirring frequently.

Mix the cabbage, onion, carrots, celery, and green pepper in a large bowl and pour the hot dressing over the vegetables. Stir and cool to room temperature. Cover with plastic wrap and refrigerate overnight.

Corn cakes

3 eggs

2½ cups fresh corn (or canned corn, drained), divided

½ cup stone-ground yellow cornmeal

1 teaspoon salt

½ teaspoon black pepper

½ cup chopped green onion

3 egg whites

2 teaspoons olive oil

Whipped goat cheese

1 cup crumbled soft goat cheese

3 tablespoons sour cream

2 teaspoons finely chopped fresh rosemary leaves (or 1 teaspoon dried)

½ teaspoon kosher salt

¼ teaspoon black pepper

Makes 12 servings

Corn Cakes with Whipped Goat Cheese

FLYING A RANCH, PINEDALE

Although the whipped goat cheese is what gives these corn cakes their unique flavor, they are delicious served without it as well.

To prepare the corn cakes:
Preheat the oven to 350 degrees. In a blender or food processor, combine the eggs and 1½ cups of corn until smooth.

Transfer to a large mixing bowl and stir in the cornmeal, salt, pepper, green onion, and remaining 1 cup of corn.

Whip the egg whites in a small mixing bowl until stiff peaks form; fold into the corn mixture.

Heat the oil in a large skillet over medium heat. Pour the batter into the skillet in ¼–cup amounts to make the cakes; cook until golden brown, about 2 minutes on each side.

Place the cooked cakes on a baking sheet and top with a dollop of the whipped goat cheese; bake until the goat cheese just begins to melt, about 5 to 10 minutes.

To prepare the whipped goat cheese:
Combine the goat cheese, sour cream, rosemary, salt, and pepper in a mixing bowl. Set aside until needed.

Salad

4 cups mixed field greens

1 Fuji apple

2 tablespoons lemon juice

¼ cup crumbled Stilton cheese

Candied pistachios

½ cup pistachios

¼ cup water

¼ cup sugar

1 sprig rosemary

Dressing

Juice and zest of 1 lime

Juice of 1 orange

2 tablespoons Dijon mustard

1 minced garlic clove

Pinch salt

Pinch cayenne pepper

¼ teaspoon extra-virgin olive oil

Makes 4 servings

Field Greens with Apple, Blue Cheese, Candied Pistachios, and Citrus Vinaigrette

RANGER CREEK GUEST RANCH, SHELL
CHEF AMANDA SCHROEDER

What a memorable first course this beautiful salad offers with its unique combination of tastes, textures, and colors. Serve with a grilled chicken or pork entrée for a stylish meal that does not require much time to prepare.

To prepare the salad:
Core the apple and cut it into eight wedges; sprinkle the apple wedges with lemon juice to prevent browning and set aside.

To prepare the candied pistachios:
Place the pistachios in a small skillet and cook over medium heat for 2 to 3 minutes to toast lightly. Remove from the heat and set aside.

Heat the water, sugar, and rosemary in a saucepan over medium heat; cook until reduced by half.

Line a baking sheet with foil and spray it lightly with cooking spray. Add the pistachios to the reduced sugar mixture and toss them gently to coat. Pour them onto the baking sheet to cool.

To prepare the dressing:
Whisk together the lime juice, lime zest, orange juice, mustard, garlic, salt, and pepper. Slowly drizzle in the olive oil, whisking constantly until combined.

Presentation:
Toss the greens with the desired amount of dressing in a large bowl. Arrange the greens on four chilled plates and top each salad with the cheese and coarsely chopped candied pistachios, with the apple wedges on the side.

Salad

9 cups fresh spinach

2 cups fresh strawberries

½ cup slivered almonds

Dressing

¼ cup canola oil

2 tablespoons sugar

2 tablespoons cider vinegar

1 tablespoon minced onion

1 teaspoon poppy seeds

1 teaspoon toasted sesame seeds

¼ teaspoon paprika

⅛ teaspoon Worcestershire sauce

Makes 6 to 8 servings

Listed on the National Register of Historic Places, the Historic Governors' Mansion in Cheyenne was home to Wyoming's first families from 1905 to 1976. A notable distinction of this beautiful mansion is that the nation's first female governor, Nellie Taylor Ross, lived there. It is now a home museum that is open to the public.

Governor's Spinach and Strawberry Salad

GOVERNOR DAVE FREUDENTHAL AND
FIRST LADY NANCY FREUDENTHAL

Freudenthal family favorite, this delicious, nutritious salad is very easy to prepare! I love the dressing, and it is excellent with a variety of other salads, too.

To prepare the salad:
Wash the spinach and remove the stems; set aside to dry. Wash the strawberries, remove the stems, and cut them into halves; set aside.

To prepare the dressing:
Combine the oil, sugar, vinegar, onion, poppy seeds, sesame seeds, paprika, and Worcestershire sauce in a blender and process until smooth.

Preparation:
In a large bowl, toss the spinach, strawberries, and almonds. Pour the dressing over the salad and toss gently to coat. Serve immediately.

(See photograph on page 35)

4 tablespoons butter

½ cup chopped onion

1 cup seeded and diced
   fresh green chiles

2 tablespoons ground cumin

2 cups heavy cream

2 cups milk

2 cups ground cornmeal

¼ cup grated Asiago cheese

Salt and freshly ground black
   pepper to taste

Makes 4 to 6 servings

Green Chile Polenta

THE HISTORIC PLAINS HOTEL, CHEYENNE
CHEF JOHN KULON

Polenta is a popular Italian dish made with dried ground cornmeal. This unique version offers a blend of ingredients that combine to create a Southwestern flair. The consistency of the polenta depends on individual preference. If you prefer a thick polenta, simply add more cornmeal; use less cornmeal for a loose mixture.

Melt the butter in a large saucepan over medium heat. Add the onion and green chiles; sauté for 2 to 3 minutes.

Stir in the cumin and cook 1 for minute, stirring frequently.

Slowly add the cream and milk; simmer for 2 minutes.

Whisk in the cornmeal and stir constantly until cooked to desired consistency.

Stir in the cheese and mix until cheese is melted.

Add the salt and pepper; serve immediately.

2 cups chopped cooked
chicken breast

¼ cup finely chopped onion

1 teaspoon dried tarragon

1 ¼ cups chopped celery

1 cup mayonnaise

½ teaspoon Old Bay seasoning

¼ cup chopped walnuts

Makes 4 servings

High Plains Chicken Salad

FIRE ROCK STEAKHOUSE AND GRILL, CASPER
CHEFS JEREMY MIDDLETON AND VICKY EASTON

This versatile salad is served at the restaurant on a peeled, pitted, and halved avocado. It is also offered as a croissant sandwich with fresh fruit on the side. I discovered that it makes a tasty sandwich wrap when rolled into a whole-wheat tortilla with chopped apple and shredded lettuce. You may substitute reduced fat mayonnaise for a low-calorie alternative.

In a large mixing bowl, combine all of the ingredients. Refrigerate for 2 hours before serving.

20 to 25 thin asparagus stalks

2 tablespoons extra-virgin olive oil

¼ cup Grand Marnier liqueur
    (or 1 tablespoon orange
    juice concentrate)

Makes 4 servings

Marinated Asparagus

RANGER CREEK GUEST RANCH, SHELL
CHEF AMANDA SCHROEDER

*I love this attractive side dish because it is elegant, delicious, and easy
to prepare. Served warm, it is the perfect accompaniment to simple beef,
chicken, fish, and seafood entrées. Note the chef uses Grand Marnier,
an orange-flavored liqueur, in this recipe; you may substitute with
Cointreau or other orange-flavored liqueur. If you prefer not to use
a liqueur, substitute orange juice concentrate.*

Rinse and trim 2 inches off the base of each asparagus stalk and
place the stalks in a baking dish.

In a small mixing bowl, whisk together the olive oil and liqueur or
orange juice concentrate; drizzle over the asparagus to evenly coat
the stalks. Set aside and marinate at room temperature for 1 hour.

Preheat the oven to 425 degrees. Transfer the asparagus to a baking
pan and arrange the stalks in a single layer. Roast the asparagus for
10 to 12 minutes, until crisp–tender, being careful not to overcook.
Remove from the oven and transfer immediately to a serving platter
to halt the cooking.

Mushroom Risotto

YELLOWSTONE NATIONAL PARK
EXECUTIVE CHEF JAMES CHAPMAN

5½ cups chicken stock or broth

2 tablespoons butter

2 minced garlic cloves

1 tablespoon minced shallots

¼ cup sliced shiitake mushrooms

¼ cup diced portabella
    mushrooms, with gills removed

1¾ cups Arborio rice

1 cup white wine

¼ cup heavy cream

¼ cup grated Parmesan cheese

1 tablespoon chopped fresh
    flatleaf parsley

Makes 4 servings

A creamy Italian rice dish, risotto is a fabulous accompaniment to a variety of beef, lamb, pork, chicken, fish, and seafood entrées.

In a medium-size pan, heat the stock or broth over medium heat; lower the heat to simmer and cover.

In a large saucepan, melt the butter over low heat; add the garlic and shallots and sauté, stirring constantly, until soft (do not brown).

Add the mushrooms and sauté for 3 minutes. Stir in the rice to coat and slowly add ½ cup stock or broth; cook over medium-low heat until dry. Repeat until remaining stock is added in ½-cup increments, about 25 minutes.

Stir in the wine, cream, Parmesan, and parsley; heat through over low heat and serve immediately.

8 strips bacon, cooked and crumbled (reserve 1 tablespoon drippings)

⅔ cup finely chopped onion

1 quart whole milk

6 tablespoons butter

1 cup uncooked quick-cook grits

1 cup Parmesan cheese

Salt and freshly ground black pepper to taste

Makes 6 servings

Onion and Bacon Grits

SWEETWATER RESTAURANT, JACKSON
OWNER/CHEF TREY DAVIS

This signature side dish reflects Chef Trey Davis's Southern roots and is served at the restaurant with Braised Buffalo Pot Roast (see the recipe in the Main Courses section).

Heat the reserved bacon drippings in a skillet and sauté the onion over medium heat until translucent, about 10 minutes.

In a separate heavy saucepan, combine the milk and butter; bring to a low boil and stir in the grits. Reduce the heat to low and cover; simmer until the grits are cooked through.

Stir in the bacon, cheese, salt, and pepper; mix well and serve warm.

½ head iceberg lettuce,
  chopped into ½-inch pieces

1 (14.5-ounce) can palm hearts,
  drained and sliced

1 (14.5-ounce) can artichoke hearts,
  drained and quartered

¼ cup grated Asiago cheese,
  divided

1 to 2 teaspoons freshly ground
  black pepper

¼ cup extra-virgin olive oil

¼ cup balsamic vinegar

Makes 8 servings

Pair of Hearts Chopped Salad

THE HISTORIC PLAINS HOTEL, CHEYENNE
CHEF JOHN KULON

The distinctive ingredients in this salad combine to create a unique medley of flavors and textures. Add thinly sliced prosciutto ham or chopped chicken for a flavorsome addition. I like to refrigerate the salad thirty minutes before serving, but do not toss with the vinaigrette until ready to serve.

Combine the chopped lettuce, palm hearts, artichoke hearts, ⅛ cup grated cheese, and pepper in a large mixing bowl. Cover with plastic wrap and refrigerate for 30 minutes.

In a separate mixing bowl, whisk together the olive oil and vinegar; pour this over the salad and toss gently when ready to serve. Garnish with remaining Asiago cheese and serve immediately.

1 medium head roasted garlic
(see recipe at right)

1 tablespoon olive oil

1 teaspoon salt

1 ½ to 2 pounds red potatoes,
peeled and cut into eighths

½ cup whole milk

4 tablespoons butter

Salt and white pepper to taste

Makes 4 to 6 servings

Harvesting Wyoming potatoes.
WYOMING STATE ARCHIVES, DEPARTMENT OF
STATE PARKS AND CULTURAL RESOURCES,
SUB NEG 18422

Roasted Garlic Mashed Potatoes

RANGER CREEK GUEST RANCH, SHELL
CHEF AMANDA SCHROEDER

When garlic is roasted, it is transformed into a sweet, caramelized puree that is the perfect addition to creamy mashed potatoes. I roast the garlic heads in batches for use in soups, sauces, and as a bread-spread as well. Each roasted garlic head makes about one tablespoon of garlic puree.

To prepare the roasted garlic:
Preheat the oven or toaster oven to 400 degrees. Drizzle the garlic (still in its peel) with olive oil and wrap it in aluminum foil. Bake until softened, about 45 to 50 minutes. Remove from the oven and cool. When ready to use, cut the end and squeeze the garlic from the outer peel (discard the peel).

To prepare the mashed potatoes:
Bring a large pot of water and salt to a boil over high heat and add the potatoes. Bring the water back to a boil and cook the potatoes until tender, about 20 minutes.

In a small saucepan, heat the milk, butter, and roasted garlic over low heat until the butter is melted.

Drain the potatoes and return them to the pot; stir in the milk, butter, and garlic mixture and mash the potatoes until creamy. Season with salt and pepper and serve immediately.

1 pound ground beef or sausage

1 pound bacon, sliced into
    ½-inch pieces

1 onion, diced into ½-inch pieces

1 (16-ounce) can pork and beans

1 (16-ounce) can kidney beans

1 (16-ounce) can lima beans

1 (16-ounce) can butter beans

½ cup brown sugar

2 tablespoons cider vinegar

1 tablespoon prepared mustard

½ cup ketchup

Salt and freshly ground
    black pepper to taste

Makes 8 to 12 servings

For President Theodore Roosevelt, an avid outdoorsman, the most unique characteristic of Yellowstone National Park was not the geysers or the abundant wildlife he saw during his visits. To him, what made the world's first national park special was that it was established "for the benefit and enjoyment of the people" and served as a symbol of democracy.

Roosevelt Beans

YELLOWSTONE NATIONAL PARK
EXECUTIVE SOUS CHEF MIKE DEAN

This historic recipe is requested so frequently by Yellowstone National Park visitors that it is printed on cards and given to guests. Once you taste these flavorsome beans, you will know why the recipe has become a treasured souvenir.

Preheat the oven to 325 degrees. In a large skillet, cook the meat and onion over medium-low heat for about 10 to 15 minutes; drain the fat.

Drain the beans and add them to the meat mixture, then stir in the sugar, vinegar, mustard, ketchup, salt, and pepper. Transfer to a baking dish and bake for 45 minutes.

Scalloped Sweet Potatoes

GAMEFISH RESTAURANT AT SNAKE RIVER LODGE AND SPA,
JACKSON HOLE ❧ EXECUTIVE CHEF KEVIN HUMPHREYS

2 pounds sweet potatoes
(about 3 medium-size potatoes)

¾ cup heavy cream

½ cup half-and-half

3 eggs

½ teaspoon ground cinnamon

¼ teaspoon ground nutmeg

1 tablespoon maple syrup

1½ teaspoons brown sugar

Salt and white pepper to taste

1 tablespoon butter

Makes 8 servings

A signature side dish at the award-winning Gamefish Restaurant, these creamy sweet potatoes are served with a grilled elk chop and apple cider reduction. This side dish is an ideal accompaniment to grilled or roasted pork and poultry.

Preheat the oven to 300 degrees. Peel the potatoes and slice them to ⅛-inch thickness.

In a medium-size mixing bowl, whisk together the cream, half-and-half, eggs, cinnamon, nutmeg, maple syrup, brown sugar, salt, and pepper. Stir in the sliced potatoes and coat them with the mixture.

Oil an 8 x 8 x 2-inch baking dish with butter and line it with the coated potatoes; pour the remaining mixture over the potatoes. Bake for 1½ hours, or until the potatoes are tender.

2 tablespoons extra-virgin olive oil

1 tablespoon minced garlic

2 teaspoons minced shallots

1 teaspoon chopped
    fresh thyme leaves

5 cups cooked white beans

¾ cup slivered sun-dried tomatoes
    (soak in water if too dry
    and drain)

⅓ cup dry white wine

1½ cups chicken stock or broth

½ cup chopped fresh basil

¼ cup minced fresh
    flat-leaf parsley

Salt and freshly ground
    black pepper to taste

Makes 6 servings

Tuscan-Style Beans with Sun-Dried Tomatoes and Fresh Herbs

OLIVER'S BAR AND GRILL, SHERIDAN
OWNER/CHEF OLIVER "MATT" WALLOP

At the restaurant, this side is served with Lamb Ossobucco (see the recipe in the Main Courses section). I love these beans with grilled chicken, too. Simply add more stock if you want to serve as a savory soup.

Place a large saucepan over medium–high heat for 2 to 3 minutes. When the pan is very hot, add the olive oil, garlic, shallots, and thyme. Stir to coat with olive oil, then add the beans and tomatoes.

Continue to cook over medium–high heat while stirring constantly, 2 to 3 minutes, being careful not to scorch.

Stir in the wine and cook for 2 more minutes.

Add the stock or broth and lower the heat; simmer the beans until most of the liquid is absorbed and the mixture is thick.

Stir in the basil, parsley, salt, and pepper. Remove from the heat and serve.

Warm Green Bean Salad with Mustard Dressing, p. 52

Salad

1 pound fresh green beans, washed and trimmed

4 medium Yukon gold potatoes

2 red bell peppers

¼ cup julienne-sliced prosciutto ham

1 cup quartered artichoke hearts in oil

Dressing

¾ cup verjus or white wine vinegar

3 tablespoons honey

1 tablespoon whole-grain mustard

1 tablespoon Dijon-style mustard

1 tablespoon dried tarragon

1 clove garlic

½ shallot

1 cooked bacon slice, finely chopped

1 cup olive oil

Salt and freshly ground black pepper to taste

Makes 6 servings

Warm Green Bean Salad with Mustard Dressing

THE PINES RESTAURANT AT TETON PINES RESORT AND COUNTRY CLUB, JACKSON HOLE   EXECUTIVE CHEF JOSEPH MCGARRY

This lively salad is prepared with a flavorful sweet dressing enhanced by verjus, a non-fermented juice made from unripened white grapes in France. You may substitute with high-quality white wine vinegar.

To prepare the salad:

Preheat the oven to 350 degrees. In a large saucepan, blanch the beans in water over high heat for 1 to 2 minutes. Transfer them to a bowl of cold water to halt cooking, then drain and set aside.

Place the potatoes and bell peppers in a 13 x 9 x 2–inch baking pan and roast them for 45 minutes; remove and let cool.

Peel and cut the potatoes into ½–inch slices. Remove the skins and seeds from the bell peppers and cut them into thin, 2-inch–long strips.

To prepare the dressing:

Combine the verjus or vinegar, honey, mustards, tarragon, garlic, shallot, and bacon. Slowly add the olive oil, salt, and pepper.

Preparation:

In the baking pan, mix the green beans, potatoes, bell peppers, prosciutto ham, and artichoke hearts; add the dressing and toss. Return to the oven for 10 to 15 minutes, or until warmed through.

(See photograph on page 51)

Salad

1 cup wild rice

4 cups chicken stock or broth

1 cup chopped cooked
    chicken breast

½ cup chopped celery

½ cup cored, peeled, and
    diced apple

½ cup dried cranberries

½ cup coarsely chopped walnuts

Dressing

⅔ cup mayonnaise

2 tablespoons whole milk

1 teaspoon lemon juice

¼ teaspoon salt

⅛ teaspoon black pepper

Makes 6 to 8 servings

Wild Rice Salad

Wild rice is not actually rice; it is a highly nutritious annual water-grass seed that was a staple of the American Indian diet. For a vegetarian alternative, or to serve as a side dish, cook the wild rice in water and omit the chicken.

To prepare the salad:
In a medium saucepan, cook the wild rice in the chicken stock or broth according to the package directions. Remove from the heat, transfer to a large mixing bowl, and cool to room temperature.

Add the chicken, celery, apple, cranberries, and walnuts. Toss with the dressing and refrigerate at least 1 hour before serving.

To prepare the dressing:
In a mixing bowl, combine the mayonnaise, milk, lemon juice, salt and pepper; add to the rice mixture and toss gently until all the ingredients are combined.

¼ pound bacon, thickly sliced
(preferably fruit-wood smoked)

½ pound carrots, peeled
and diced

½ pound parsnips, peeled
and diced

2 sprigs rosemary, freshly chopped
(or ½ teaspoon dried)

2 sprigs thyme, freshly chopped
(or ½ teaspoon dried)

2 sage leaves, freshly chopped
(or ½ teaspoon dried)

½ pound onions, peeled and diced

Salt and freshly ground black
pepper to taste

Makes 4 to 6 servings

Winter Root Vegetable Hash

THE GRANARY RESTAURANT AT SPRING CREEK RANCH, JACKSON
EXECUTIVE CHEF JASON MITCHELL

*A generous medley of herbs adds depth and contrast to this hearty side dish,
so use fresh herbs if possible.*

Preheat the oven to 400 degrees. Cut the bacon into small pieces and
cook over medium heat in an oven-safe pan or cast-iron skillet.

When the bacon begins to crisp, add the carrots, parsnips, and
herbs. Cook over medium-low heat, stirring occasionally to coat
the vegetables in rendered bacon fat, for about 5 minutes.

Add the onions and cook over medium-low heat for another
5 minutes.

Stir in the salt and pepper; transfer the pan or skillet to the oven
and roast for 20 to 30 minutes, or until the vegetables are softened
and lightly browned.

Soups & Stews

Minestrone Soup with Parmigiano-Reggiano Croutons, p. 65

2 tablespoons olive oil

3 to 4 pounds trimmed, boneless
    lamb shoulder, cut into
    1-inch cubes

1½ cups chopped Spanish onion

1 cup chopped red bell pepper

6 garlic cloves, peeled and crushed

1 cup peeled, seeded, and
    coarsely chopped tomato
    with liquid

½ cup dry white wine

1 teaspoon dried thyme leaves

1 teaspoon dried rosemary leaves

1 teaspoon paprika

Salt and freshly ground black
    pepper to taste

1 cup chicken stock or broth

1 bay leaf

Makes 6 to 8 servings

Basque Lamb Stew

Wyoming is home to a number of descendants of the Basque people from Spain and France who immigrated to the Cowboy State during the mid- to late 1800s. This savory dish is representative of simple Basque culinary fare, which usually features lamb and garlic. You may prepare this dish in a slow cooker as well, after browning the meat.

In a Dutch oven or 4-quart soup pot, heat the olive oil over medium-high heat.

Add the lamb in small batches. Brown the meat on all sides, about 10 minutes; remove the lamb with a slotted spoon. Repeat the process until all the lamb is browned and then set aside.

Add the onion, red bell pepper, and crushed garlic to the pan; lower the heat to medium-low and cook until the onion and bell pepper are soft, about 5 minutes, stirring occasionally to avoid browning.

Stir in the tomato, wine, thyme, rosemary, paprika, salt, and pepper. Bring to a low boil over high heat, then reduce the heat to medium-low and simmer to reduce and thicken, about 15 minutes.

Stir in the chicken stock or broth, the lamb, and the bay leaf; cover, and simmer over low heat for 2 to 2½ hours, stirring occasionally. Add more stock if additional liquid is needed.

Soup

3 tablespoons olive oil

4 tablespoons butter

2 cups lardons (small dice, thick-cut bacon)

1 ½ cups finely chopped onion

1 cup finely chopped celery

1 cup finely chopped carrots

2 tablespoons chopped garlic

3 quarts canned tomatoes (equal to one #10 can)

8 cups chicken stock

Salt and freshly ground black pepper to taste

Croutons

1 tablespoon butter

2 tablespoons olive oil

3 slices sourdough bread, cut into ½-inch cubes

Salt and freshly ground black pepper to taste

Makes 10 to 12 servings

BLT Soup with Sourdough Croutons, Crispy Bacon Lardons, and Arugula Pesto

TRIO, JACKSON
OWNERS/CHEFS WILL BRADOF, BEAU LITTLE, AND PAUL WIREMAN

This recipe makes a large batch of one of Trio's superb signature menu items. Simply reduce the ingredients by half if you want to make less. Never heard of lardons? They are small pieces of bacon cut into cubes. In order to serve immediately following preparation, I prepare the garnishes first and then the soup.

To prepare the soup:
In a large stockpot, heat the olive oil and butter until foaming over medium–high heat.

Add the onion, celery, carrots, and garlic and cook over medium heat until translucent.

Stir in the tomatoes and chicken stock; lower the heat, cover, and simmer for 10 to 15 minutes.

Remove from the heat, add salt and pepper, and blend to puree.

To prepare the croutons:
Preheat the oven to 375 degrees. Melt the butter and mix with the olive oil in a large bowl; add the bread cubes, salt, and pepper and gently toss until the bread is coated.

Transfer to a large baking sheet and bake for 8 minutes, or until golden brown.

(continued page 58)

Lardons

1 ¼ pounds sliced bacon

Pesto

1 cup arugula

½ cup spinach

1 ¾ cup olive oil

1 ½ cup Parmesan cheese

1 tablespoon toasted pine nuts

Salt and freshly ground
    black pepper to taste

To prepare the lardons:
Dice the bacon into small pieces. Heat a heavy-bottomed skillet over medium heat; cook the bacon until the fat has rendered off and the bacon is crispy.

To prepare the pesto:
Combine the arugula, spinach, olive oil, cheese, pine nuts, salt, and pepper in a blender or food processor and puree until smooth.

Presentation:
Ladle the soup into bowls and top with 1 teaspoon of pesto, then the bacon and croutons.

PUBLISHED BY THE UNIVERSITY
OF UTAH PRESS IN 1999

FROM *WHERE RIVERS CHANGE DIRECTION*
BY MARK SPRAGG

The sun has topped the east ridge, and morning light falls and stands through the timber like a scatter of quarried granite. Wyoming light. Mountain light. I press down with my toes and arch my feet against the boots' insteps. It is the first week in June. I have read in Black Elk's book that the Oglala Sioux called this time of year the Moon of Making Fat. I grip the taut flesh at my belly. I am full of sausage, eggs, bread, potatoes. I feel weighty, fueled for the morning. I look again at my boots. I press my weight down into them.

Seasoned broth

2 quarts chicken broth

1 medium onion, diced

2 celery stalks, chopped

2 carrots, peeled and diced

1 tablespoon dark chili powder

2 teaspoons smoked paprika

2 teaspoons dried cumin

1 teaspoon dried thyme leaves

1 teaspoon dried oregano

1 teaspoon granulated garlic

Pinch red pepper or hot sauce
    (optional)

Jalapeño pepper, seeded and
    chopped (optional)

Soup

2 blue corn tortillas

2 to 3 tablespoons canola oil

2 quarts seasoned broth
    (see recipe)

2 cups diced grilled chicken breast

½ cup fresh or canned corn

32 grape tomatoes, halved

2 avocados, peeled, pitted,
    quartered, and sliced

½ cup grated pepper Jack cheese

¼ cup finely chopped cilantro

Salt and freshly ground black
    pepper to taste

Makes 8 servings

Blue Corn Tortilla Soup

THE HISTORIC PLAINS HOTEL, CHEYENNE ❧ CHEF JOHN KULON

This colorful soup has a delicious variety of ingredients, and it comes together quickly. Although this is a simple and uncomplicated recipe, it does not compromise on flavor. Serve with warm tortillas or tortilla chips and salsa on the side for a filling lunch or dinner.

To prepare the seasoned broth:
Combine the broth, onion, celery, carrots, chili powder, paprika, cumin, thyme, oregano, and garlic in a saucepan and bring to a boil; lower the heat and simmer for 15 minutes, partially covered. Remove from the heat and strain. Discard onion, celery, and carrots and add the soup ingredients according to the instructions below.

To prepare the soup:
Cut the tortillas in half and slice them into thin strips, about ¼-inch wide.

Heat the oil over medium-high heat in a skillet and cook the tortilla strips on both sides until crispy, stirring frequently. Remove them from the pan and set aside on paper towels.

Heat the prepared broth in a saucepan over medium-high heat. Add the chicken and corn; lower the heat to simmer until warmed through.

Ladle into large soup bowls and distribute even portions of tortilla strips, tomato, avocado, cheese, and cilantro into the bowls. Season with salt and pepper; serve immediately.

2 tablespoons canola oil

2 pounds beef stew meat

¾ cup chopped onion

¾ cup chopped green bell pepper

1 tablespoon all-purpose flour

3 (15¼ -ounce) cans dark
    kidney beans (drain and
    reserve liquid)

1 (10¾ -ounce) can tomato puree

½ cup water

2 to 3 garlic cloves, minced

2 tablespoons chili powder

1 teaspoon paprika

½ teaspoon ground cumin

Salt and freshly ground black
    pepper to taste

Pinch red pepper (optional)

Optional garnishes

Grated cheddar cheese

Chopped white or green onion

Chopped jalapeño peppers

Makes 6 to 8 servings

Branding Day Chili

CAMERON RANCH, RIVERTON

Cameron Ranch is a Wyoming working ranch that specializes in grass-fed beef and lamb. An authentic Western favorite, this thick, zesty chili is baked in the oven, allowing the ingredients to meld together. You may prepare the chili in a slow cooker after browning the beef, if desired. Serve this traditional chili with a green salad and skillet corn bread for a hearty meal.

Preheat the oven to 325 degrees. Heat the oil over medium heat in a large flame- and ovenproof crock; cook the beef until lightly browned.

Add the onion and green bell pepper; cook until just tender, about 10 minutes.

Sprinkle the flour over the beef mixture and mix until the flour is absorbed.

Stir in the reserved liquid from the beans, the tomato puree, water, and seasonings. Cover and bake for 1½ to 2 hours. Stir occasionally and, if the chili is too thick, add more water to achieve the desired consistency.

Remove from the oven, add the beans, cover, and return to the oven for 20 to 25 minutes, until the beans are warmed through.

1 tablespoon olive oil

½ cup finely chopped onion

3 cups chicken stock or broth

1 cup water

1 ½ pounds peeled, diced
    butternut squash

¼ cup seeded and finely
    chopped jalapeño peppers

2 cups heavy cream

Pinch ground nutmeg

½ teaspoon kosher salt

½ teaspoon freshly ground
    black pepper

Makes 6 servings

Butternut Squash and Jalapeño Soup

ALTITUDE CHOPHOUSE AND BREWERY, LARAMIE

The unexpected addition of jalapeño peppers to this rich, creamy soup provides a pleasant contrast to the mild flavor of the squash, and it does not overwhelm the palate with too much heat.

Heat the oil in a large pan on medium heat; sauté the onion until translucent.

Add the chicken stock or broth and the water; bring to a boil and add the squash. Lower the heat to medium and cover; cook until the squash is tender, about 10 to 15 minutes.

Stir in the peppers and cream. Bring to a low boil, then remove from the heat and cool for 20 to 30 minutes.

Transfer to a blender or food processor and puree. Pour the soup through a strainer, then add seasonings. Return to the pan and warm over low heat. Ladle into soup bowls and serve immediately.

4 tablespoons butter

1 cauliflower head, coarsely chopped

1 fennel bulb, coarsely chopped

½ cup chopped onion

½ cup chopped celery

½ cup Sambuca liqueur (or 1 to 2 tablespoons anise extract)

8 cups vegetable stock or broth

1 cup heavy cream

Salt and white pepper to taste

Makes 4 to 6 servings

Cauliflower and Fennel Soup

JENNY LAKE LODGE, JACKSON HOLE
EXECUTIVE CHEF JOSHUA CONRAD

Served with one of the fabulous five-course dinners at Jenny Lake Lodge, this creamy, refined soup is a favorite of mine. Sambuca, a sweet Italian liqueur, infuses this velvety soup with a subtle licorice flavor. Anise extract may be used as a substitute for the liqueur in the quantity noted.

Melt the butter in a large stockpot and add the cauliflower, fennel, onion, and celery; sauté over low heat until tender, about 10 minutes.

Add the liqueur or extract and deglaze the pan over medium heat, stirring constantly for about 3 to 4 minutes.

Add the stock or broth and bring to a boil; lower the heat and simmer partially covered for 15 to 20 minutes.

Remove from the heat and let cool for 10 minutes. Puree in batches in a blender or food processor until smooth.

Return the mixture to the stockpot and stir in the cream, salt, and pepper. Simmer over low heat until warmed through.

½ cup butter

2 medium Spanish onions, chopped

2 large red onions, sliced

4 leeks, chopped (white part only)

1 bunch (8 to 10) green onions, chopped (white part and 1-inch of green)

2 shallots, sliced

1 ½ quarts chicken stock or broth

⅓ cup brandy

¼ cup whiskey

½ cup heavy cream

Salt and freshly ground black pepper to taste

Makes 4 to 6 servings

Five-Onion Soup

REMINGTON'S RESTAURANT AT THE POWDER HORN GOLF CLUBHOUSE, SHERIDAN   ❧   CHEF TIM ROCKWELL

If you are a fan of onion soup, you'll love this creamy blend of onions that offers a mélange of flavors. Serve with warm, thick slices of French bread or baguettes.

Melt the butter in a large, heavy–bottomed stockpot or saucepan over low heat; add the Spanish and red onions. Increase the heat to medium and sauté the onions until they begin to turn golden brown, stirring frequently, about 8 minutes.

Add the leeks, the white part of the green onions, and shallots; sauté over medium–low heat, stirring frequently until tender.

Stir in the stock or broth, brandy, and whiskey. Bring to a boil, reduce the heat, and simmer partially covered for 1 hour.

Add the green part of the green onions; remove from the heat and cool slightly. Slowly stir in the cream. Add the salt and pepper, cover, and refrigerate overnight.

Reheat over medium–low heat, being careful not to scorch, and serve hot.

Soup

½ cup julienne-sliced
    prosciutto ham

3 tablespoons olive oil

1 cup chopped yellow onion

2 tablespoons minced garlic

2 cups diced tomatoes

1 cup diced zucchini

½ cup diced yellow squash

8 cups chicken stock or broth

2 cups cannellini beans

1 cup wilted spinach

1 cup cooked small macaroni
    pasta (½ cup uncooked)

2 tablespoons Parmigiano-
    Reggiano cheese

1 tablespoon fresh basil
    (1 teaspoon dried)

1 tablespoon fresh oregano
    (1 teaspoon dried)

Salt and freshly ground black
    pepper to taste

Croutons

1 pound grated Jarlsberg
    Swiss cheese

¼ cup Parmigiano-
    Reggiano cheese

½ cup all-purpose flour

½ teaspoon baking powder

1 tablespoon freshly chopped
    flat-leaf parsley

6 eggs

Makes 8 servings

Minestrone Soup with Parmigiano-Reggiano Croutons

THE PINES RESTAURANT AT TETON PINES RESORT AND COUNTRY CLUB, JACKSON HOLE ❧ EXECUTIVE CHEF JOSEPH MCGARRY

This version of the traditional Italian soup laden with pasta, beans, and vegetables includes strips of prosciutto, a dry-cured Italian ham. The chef suggests cutting the vegetables and croutons into half-inch pieces. Store any extra croutons in an airtight container for up to one week; they're wonderful on salads.

To prepare the soup:
Sauté the prosciutto in a large stockpot over medium–high heat for 3 to 4 minutes.

Add the olive oil and onion; sauté the onion until translucent, stirring frequently.

Stir in the garlic, tomatoes, zucchini, and yellow squash; cook over high heat until the vegetables are tender, about 5 minutes.

Add the stock or broth and bring to a boil; stir in the beans, spinach, cooked pasta, cheese, basil, oregano, salt, and pepper. Sprinkle with croutons and serve hot.

To prepare the croutons:
Preheat the oven to 350 degrees. Beat the eggs in a mixing bowl until foamy; set aside to rest.

In a separate mixing bowl, combine the cheeses, flour, baking powder, and parsley. Pour the eggs into the cheese mixture and combine well.

Heavily coat a baking pan with oil or cooking spray; spread the mixture on the baking pan and bake for 25 to 30 minutes. Remove from the oven, cool for 10 to 15 minutes, and cut into small cubes.

(See photograph on page 55)

6 tablespoons butter, divided

1 medium onion, peeled and diced

4 carrots, peeled and diced

4 celery stalks, with leaves, diced

1 green bell pepper, seeded
    and diced

½ head green cabbage,
    coarsely chopped

1 cup peeled and chopped apple

1½ cups diced uncooked chicken

⅓ cup all-purpose flour

1 tablespoon curry powder

½ teaspoon ground nutmeg

½ teaspoon ground cloves

6 cups chicken stock or broth

4 cups peeled chopped tomatoes

Salt and freshly ground black
    pepper to taste

Sliced toasted almonds (optional)

Makes 6 to 8 servings

Mulligatawny Soup

ANN SIMPSON, CODY

This classic Anglo-Indian soup is a family favorite shared by Ann Simpson and Alan K. Simpson, former United States senator from Wyoming. Mulligatawny is an Indian word that means "pepper water." There are as many variations of this soup as there are stories of its origin, and, like this one, many Western versions omit the hot pepper. Mrs. Simpson serves this soup with steamed white rice and sliced cold bananas on the side, creating the ultimate comfort food for her family.

Melt 4 tablespoons of the butter in a large stockpot. Add the onion, carrots, celery, bell pepper, cabbage, apple, and chicken. Sauté over medium–low heat for 10 to 15 minutes, until the vegetables are tender and the chicken is cooked, and then add the remaining 2 tablespoons butter.

In a small mixing bowl, whisk together the flour, curry powder, nutmeg, and cloves; stir into the vegetable and chicken mixture.

Stir in the stock or broth, tomatoes, salt, and pepper. Stir to combine the ingredients and simmer over low heat for 45 minutes. Ladle into soup bowls and garnish with sliced almonds if desired.

4 cups diced unpeeled red potatoes

4 tablespoons butter

1 cup finely chopped onion

1 cup finely chopped celery

2 to 3 garlic cloves, minced

¾ cup all-purpose flour

2 (10-ounce) cans clams, chopped and drained (reserve liquid)

1 quart half-and-half

4 tablespoons freshly chopped flat-leaf parsley

2 teaspoons Old Bay seasoning

½ teaspoon dried thyme leaves

Salt and freshly ground black pepper to taste

Dash hot pepper sauce (optional)

Makes 6 servings

New West Clam Chowder

WALDORF A'STORY AT PINEY CREEK GENERAL STORE, STORY

East meets west with a spicy twist on traditional New England clam chowder. Served with skillet corn bread, a hot bowl of this thick, creamy chowder on a snowy winter day will warm you from the inside out.

In a medium saucepan, parboil the potatoes in their skins for about 10 minutes. Remove from the heat, drain (reserving liquid), and set aside.

Melt the butter in a stockpot. Sauté the onion, celery, and garlic over low heat until translucent.

Add the flour and cook for 3 minutes, stirring constantly.

Slowly whisk in ½ cup of liquid reserved from the clams and ½ cup of liquid reserved from the potatoes and cook over medium heat until the mixture begins to thicken.

Stir in the half-and-half and bring to a low boil, stirring constantly.

Reduce the heat to a simmer and add the clams, potatoes, and remaining seasonings. Cover and simmer over low heat until heated thoroughly, about 10 minutes. Ladle into soup bowls and serve immediately.

2 tablespoons canola oil

1 ½ pounds trimmed pork loin,
cut into 1-inch cubes

1 cup chopped onion

2 to 3 garlic cloves, minced

6 cups chicken stock or broth

1 cup diced yellow squash

1 (14.5-ounce) can pinto beans,
drained and rinsed

1 (14.5-ounce) can black beans,
drained and rinsed

1 (14.5-ounce) can chopped
tomatoes

1 (14.5-ounce) can creamed corn

1 (7-ounce) can chopped roasted
green chiles

½ cup freshly chopped cilantro

1 teaspoon ground cumin

Salt and freshly ground black
pepper to taste

Makes 4 to 6 servings

Three Sisters Stew

I was inspired to create this savory stew after tasting a similar version in a local restaurant. To save time, prepare the stew in a slow cooker after browning the meat. If you like pepper-heat, add a seeded and finely chopped jalapeño pepper. Serve with American Indian Fry Bread on the side (see the recipe in the Appetizers and Snacks section).

Heat the oil in a large saucepan over medium–high heat and lightly brown the meat. Remove the meat from the pan with a slotted spoon and set aside.

Add the onion and sauté until translucent, about 5 minutes. Stir in the garlic and sauté for an additional 1 to 2 minutes.

Return the meat to the pan and add the stock or broth and the squash. Bring to a boil and reduce the heat to low; cover and simmer for 30 minutes.

Stir in the beans, tomatoes, creamed corn, and green chiles; cook uncovered over medium heat for 35 to 40 minutes, or until thickened to desired consistency. Stir in the cilantro, cumin, salt, and pepper and serve hot.

The name "Wyoming" originated with the Lenape tribe in the northeastern United States; it is an anglicized version of the Lenape word *Maughwauwane*, which means "great plains." The native nomadic peoples of the Great Plains were known as the Plains Indians. Three staples of the Plains Indians' diet included corn, beans, and squash; for many Indian people, this trinity was called the Three Sisters.

Venison Stew

2 pounds venison, trimmed and
cut into 1-inch cubes

½ cup all-purpose flour

4 tablespoons canola oil

1 cup chopped onion

1 teaspoon dried rosemary

3 tablespoons freshly chopped
flat-leaf parsley (or
1½ tablespoons dried)

1 tablespoon paprika

6 cups hot water

1 cup red wine

1 cup fresh or frozen, thawed peas

Salt to taste

½ teaspoon white pepper

Makes 4 to 6 servings

Venison, or deer meat, has become more popular because it has a lower fat content than beef and pork, and its availability has increased as well. You can substitute the venison with beef stew meat; prepare the stew in a slow cooker after the meat is browned.

Dredge the meat in flour.

Heat the oil in a Dutch oven and brown the meat evenly on all sides over medium heat.

Add the onion, rosemary, parsley, paprika, and water to cover the meat. Bring to a boil, then reduce the heat and simmer uncovered until the liquid thickens, about 30 minutes, stirring often.

Add the wine and simmer an additional 30 minutes over low heat. Stir in the peas, salt, and pepper. Cover and simmer for 10 minutes over low heat.

Main
Courses

Trout Almondine, p. 96

2 pounds trimmed boneless beef chuck, cut into 1-inch cubes

¼ cup all-purpose flour

6 tablespoons butter, divided

1 cup diced celery

1 cup diced carrots

1 cup diced onion

3 to 6 tablespoons coarsely chopped garlic

1 tablespoon fresh thyme leaves (or 1 teaspoon dried)

2 cups dry red wine, such as burgundy or cabernet

3 cups beef stock or broth

2 slices bacon, diced

1 cup frozen white pearl onions, thawed

8 ounces button mushrooms, wiped clean and halved

Makes 6 servings

Beef Bourguignonne

RENDEZVOUS BISTRO, JACKSON
OWNER/CHEF ROGER FREEDMAN

A hearty, robust French stew, this classic dish will delight even the most discerning diners. Serve over pasta or new potatoes with thick slices of freshly baked French bread and a mixed green salad topped with crumbled blue cheese.

Preheat the oven to 325 degrees. Lightly dust the beef cubes with flour.

In a Dutch oven, melt 2 tablespoons of butter and sear half the beef cubes over medium-high heat until evenly browned; repeat for the remaining beef. Remove the beef from the pan with a slotted spoon and set aside.

Add 2 tablespoons of butter to the Dutch oven, along with the celery, carrots, onion, garlic, and thyme; cook over medium heat for about 5 to 8 minutes.

Add the wine and cook over medium-high heat until reduced by half, stirring frequently, about 10 minutes.

Add the stock or broth and the browned beef. Bring to a boil, cover, and transfer to the oven. Cook in the oven for 1½ to 2 hours, until the meat and vegetables are tender.

Sauté the bacon in a skillet over medium heat for 4 minutes. Add the pearl onions and mushrooms; lower the heat and continue cooking for about 10 minutes, stirring frequently.

After the meat and vegetables have cooked for 1½ to 2 hours, add the bacon, onions, and mushrooms to the beef mixture and return the Dutch oven to the stove. Bring to a boil, reduce the heat, and simmer uncovered for 15 to 20 minutes.

Serve over cooked pasta, steamed rice, or boiled new potatoes tossed in butter and freshly chopped flat-leaf parsley.

Bill's Buffalo Lasagna

THE IRMA HOTEL, CODY   CHEF GARY SCHOOK

1 pound ground buffalo meat

2 tablespoons olive oil, divided

½ cup chopped onion

2 cups ricotta cheese

2 cups shredded mozzarella
cheese, divided

⅓ cup freshly grated
Parmesan cheese

2 tablespoons dried Italian
seasoning

2 tablespoons dried oregano,
divided

Salt and pepper to taste

1 (8-ounce package) dried
lasagna pasta

4 cups (or 32-ounce jar)
marinara sauce, divided

Makes 6 to 8 servings

Listed on the National Register of Historic Places, the Irma Hotel was built in 1902 by William F. Cody, who is known as the legendary Buffalo Bill and for whom the town of Cody is named. The Irma Hotel is named after his daughter, and he referred to it as "the sweetest hotel that ever was." One of the most popular entrées on the hotel dining room menu is this classic Italian-American lasagna recipe that is made with ground buffalo meat, a low-fat alternative to ground beef. Italian seasoning is a blend of herbs available at most markets.

Preheat the oven to 350 degrees. In a large skillet, cook the ground buffalo meat in 1 tablespoon of olive oil over medium heat for 5 to 7 minutes, or until lightly browned. Remove the drippings and add the onion to the skillet; cook with the meat for 5 minutes or until the onion has softened, stirring frequently (add another tablespoon of olive oil if needed). Remove from the heat and set aside.

In a large mixing bowl, combine the ricotta cheese, 1 cup of mozzarella cheese, the Italian seasoning, 1 tablespoon of oregano, and salt and pepper to taste. Add the cooked meat and mix well.

Cook the pasta according to the package directions. Use the remaining tablespoon of olive oil to coat a 13 x 9 x 3–inch baking pan and spread about ½ cup of the marinara sauce evenly in the bottom of the pan. Place three pasta pieces lengthwise in a single layer over the sauce. Spread a layer of the meat and cheese mixture over the pasta; add about 1 cup of marinara sauce and spread evenly. Repeat the process and top with the remaining sauce, 1 cup of mozzarella cheese, 1 tablespoon of oregano, and the Parmesan cheese.

Bake 35 to 40 minutes, or until the cheese is golden brown. Remove from the oven and let rest for 10 minutes before serving.

Meat

6 (6-ounce) bison tenderloins

¼ cup olive oil

Salt and freshly ground black
  pepper to taste

Sauce

½ cup white wine

1 tablespoon minced shallots

2 cups heavy cream

¼ cup crumbled blue cheese

Makes 6 servings

Bison Tenderloin with Blue Cheese Sauce

ALPENROSE RESTAURANT AT THE ALPENHOF LODGE, JACKSON HOLE
EXECUTIVE CHEF MICHAEL HOFFMAN

The American bison is commonly referred to as "buffalo" in Western culture. Bison tastes similar to beef but has a richer, sweeter flavor and a lower fat content. Because it is prepared in the same manner as beef, you can substitute beef tenderloin and serve with this lavish sauce.

To prepare the meat:
Rub both sides of the tenderloin with olive oil and season with salt and pepper. Grill the meat over medium-high heat to desired doneness.

To prepare the sauce:
In a medium saucepan, heat the wine and shallots over medium-low heat until reduced by 75 percent, about 20 to 25 minutes.

Slowly stir in the cream and continue to cook over medium-low heat until the sauce has reached a thick, heavy consistency.

Add the blue cheese and cook over low heat, stirring constantly, until the cheese has melted.

Presentation:
Place the tenderloins on warm dinner plates and spoon a small amount of sauce around each one.

2 tablespoons olive oil

3 pounds bison roast

1 onion, coarsely chopped

4 carrots, peeled and coarsely
    chopped

2 stalks celery, diced

1 bay leaf

Salt and freshly ground black
    pepper to taste

2 tablespoons tomato paste

1 cup dry red wine

1 cup beef stock or broth

1 to 2 tablespoons
    all-purpose flour

Makes 4 to 6 servings

Braised Buffalo Pot Roast

SWEETWATER RESTAURANT, JACKSON
OWNER/CHEF TREY DAVIS

A Louisiana native, Chef Trey Davis infuses his Southern heritage into this savory bison roast by serving it with Onion and Bacon Grits (see the recipe in the Salads and Sides section). For a traditional pot roast, add six peeled and quartered boiler potatoes to the Dutch oven after the roast has cooked for one hour.

To prepare the roast:

Preheat the oven to 300 degrees. In a Dutch oven, heat the oil over medium heat. Add the roast and brown it evenly on all sides.

Add the onion, carrots, celery, bay leaf, salt, and pepper; sauté to lightly brown, about 1 minute.

Stir in the tomato paste, red wine, and stock or broth; cook over medium heat for 1 minute, stirring the vegetables around the roast to deglaze the pan. Cover and cook in the oven for 2 to 2½ hours. Transfer the roast and vegetables with a slotted spoon to a warm serving platter.

To prepare the gravy:

Place the Dutch oven over a burner on medium heat. Add 1 to 2 tablespoons of all-purpose flour to the drippings and whisk for several minutes to cook the flour. If additional liquid is needed, gradually add more stock to achieve the desired consistency.

Pork loin

½ cup chopped dried apricots

1 cup Calvados brandy or
    apple juice

3 tablespoons olive oil

2 tablespoons minced onion

1 tablespoon minced garlic

1 tablespoon minced shallots

1 pound trimmed pork loin,
    cut into 2 (8-ounce) pieces

Salt and freshly ground black
    pepper to taste

2 cups freshly chopped spinach

¼ cup shredded Gruyère cheese

2 tablespoons grated Pecorino
    Romano cheese

Glaze

1 tablespoon minced shallots

1 tablespoon minced garlic

1 tablespoon herbs de Provence

1 cup port wine

1 cup demi-glaze or beef stock

4 tablespoons butter

Makes 2 servings

Brandied Apricot-Stuffed Pork Loin with Port Wine Glaze

MAMMOTH HOT SPRINGS, YELLOWSTONE NATIONAL PARK
CHEF JASON JOHNSON

Enjoy this French-inspired entrée by using Calvados, a premier apple brandy from France; you may also substitute with apple juice.

To prepare the pork loin:
Preheat the oven to 350 degrees. Combine the apricots and brandy or juice in a small saucepan and cook over medium heat until it is reduced to a thick consistency. Remove from the heat and set aside.

Heat the olive oil in a saucepan over medium heat and sauté the onion, garlic, shallots, salt, and pepper until the mixture begins to brown; stir in the spinach and continue to sauté over medium heat until the spinach wilts.

Butterfly the pork steaks by slicing the steaks in half lengthwise to open, but do not cut through and do not flatten. Season with salt and pepper.

Open each steak and spread half of the brandied apricots inside each steak; follow by filling each steak with half of the spinach mixture and half of each cheese. Fold the top half of the pork over and press firmly to hold the filling in place.

Transfer to a baking pan and roast for 45 to 50 minutes.

To prepare the glaze:
Combine the shallots, garlic, herbs, and wine in a small saucepan and cook over medium-high heat until almost completely reduced.

Add the demi-glaze or stock and continue to cook over medium-high heat until reduced by one-third. Turn off the heat and whisk the butter into the mixture. Strain and serve immediately over the pork loin.

Cedar Plank Salmon
with Walnut Beurre Blanc

ALTITUDE CHOPHOUSE AND BREWERY, LARAMIE

Cooking on a wood plank is an ancient culinary method that originated with Pacific Northwest natives. Plank cooking allows the food to retain moisture and imparts a subtle, smoky flavor. Prepare the beurre blanc ("white butter" in French) a few hours ahead of baking the salmon because it requires refrigeration prior to serving.

Beurre blanc

1 cup dry white wine

1 tablespoon minced shallots

½ cup heavy cream

1 cup butter, cut into 1-inch pieces

⅛ cup chopped walnuts

¼ teaspoon kosher salt

¼ teaspoon freshly ground
    black pepper

Salmon

6 (7-ounce) salmon fillets

Kosher salt and freshly ground
    black pepper to taste

6 sprigs of fresh rosemary

Makes 6 servings

To prepare the beurre blanc:
Heat the wine and shallots in a medium saucepan over high heat. Bring to a boil and lower the heat; simmer until reduced to about ¼ cup.

Slowly add the cream and butter to the mixture while stirring constantly. Stir in the chopped walnuts, salt, and pepper.

Remove from the heat, let cool, and refrigerate until the sauce becomes solid.

To prepare the salmon:
Preheat the oven to 400 degrees. Rinse the salmon fillets and pat them dry. Season both sides of the fillets with kosher salt and pepper.

Place the salmon on a cedar plank and bake for 20 minutes, or to preferred doneness.

Place the salmon fillets on warm plates and top each fillet with 2 tablespoons of beurre blanc. Garnish with fresh rosemary and serve immediately.

Chicken

2 (8- to10-ounce) whole boneless,
skinless chicken breasts,
cut into halves

½ cup all-purpose flour

1½ cups ground toasted hazelnuts

½ cup bread crumbs

3 eggs, beaten

4 tablespoons butter or canola oil

Sauce

¾ cup Frangelico liqueur

¼ cup chicken stock

2½ tablespoons orange juice
concentrate

1 (11-ounce can) mandarin
oranges, liquid reserved

2 teaspoons thyme leaves

¾ cup heavy cream

Makes 4 servings

Chicken Frangelico

THE BLUE LION RESTAURANT, JACKSON
CHEF TIM LIBASSI

An elegant, aromatic dish, this is a guest favorite at the charming Blue Lion Restaurant. Serve with linguini or fettuccini and delight your guests with this classic.

To prepare the chicken:
Rinse, pat dry, and lightly pound the chicken breasts. Lightly dust the chicken with flour, shaking off the excess.

Combine the hazelnuts and bread crumbs in a shallow bowl.

In a separate mixing bowl, whisk the eggs; dip the chicken into the eggs, then roll the chicken in the hazelnut–bread crumb mixture.

In a large saucepan, heat the butter or oil over medium–high heat and brown the chicken on both sides, about 10 minutes; remove from the pan and set aside, keeping warm.

To prepare the sauce:
Add the liqueur to the saucepan and cook over high heat to deglaze and burn off the alcohol.

Add the stock, orange juice concentrate, reserved liquid from the mandarin oranges, and thyme; cook over medium–high heat until the liquid is nearly evaporated, stirring constantly to avoid burning.

Add the heavy cream and cook over low heat until reduced to a smooth, thick sauce.

Stir in the oranges, heat through about 2 to 3 minutes, and remove from the heat. Serve the sauce over the chicken breasts with pasta.

The Grand Tetons and the Snake River

Meat loaf

2 pounds ground beef

2 eggs, beaten

1 ½ cups white bread crumbs

1 ½ cups whole milk

¼ cup spicy steak sauce

¼ cup finely chopped green
bell pepper

¼ cup finely chopped red bell
pepper

¼ cup finely chopped
yellow onion

1 teaspoon minced garlic

1 teaspoon dried thyme

Salt and freshly ground black
pepper to taste

Fire Rock sauce

¼ cup barbeque sauce

1 (14.5-ounce) can beef stock
or broth

1 tablespoon powdered beef base

Makes 6 servings

Fire Rock Meat Loaf

FIRE ROCK STEAKHOUSE AND GRILL, CASPER
CHEFS JEREMY MIDDLETON AND VICKY EASTON

*At the restaurant, this spicy signature dish is served with Onion Straws
(see the recipe in the Appetizers and Snacks section). Prepare the Fire Rock
sauce while the meat loaf is baking and keep the sauce warm in the oven
until ready to serve.*

To prepare the meat loaf:
Preheat the oven to 350 degrees. In a large mixing bowl, combine
the beef, eggs, bread crumbs, milk, steak sauce, peppers, onion,
garlic, thyme, salt, and pepper until mixed well.

Transfer to a large loaf pan, cover with foil, and bake for 1 hour.
Remove from the oven and top with the Fire Rock sauce. Return
to the oven and bake uncovered for 10 minutes.

To prepare the Fire Rock sauce:
Combine the barbeque sauce, stock or broth, and beef base in a
medium saucepan and cook over low heat until the sauce thickens,
stirring occasionally, about 20 to 30 minutes. Serve extra sauce on
the side.

Chicken

1 whole chicken, split and
cut for frying

2 cups all-purpose flour

1 ½ teaspoons ground thyme

1 ½ teaspoons ground sage

1 ½ teaspoons ground tarragon

Salt and freshly ground black
pepper to taste

1 to 2 cups canola oil

Cream gravy

4 tablespoons butter

¾ cup chicken livers,
rinsed and dried

¼ cup minced onion

4 tablespoons all-purpose flour

½ cup dry white wine

1 ½ cups chicken stock or broth

2 cups heavy cream

Salt and black pepper to taste

Makes 4 to 6 servings

Fried Spring Chicken
with Cream Gravy

YELLOWSTONE NATIONAL PARK HISTORIC RECIPE, JULY 4, 1947

I can imagine the festive, patriotic atmosphere in which the guests enjoyed this all-American entrée at the world's first national park on Independence Day in 1947, only two years after the end of World War II. This delicious traditional dish is the perfect choice for a family picnic in the park.

To prepare the chicken:
Wash the chicken pieces and pat them dry.

Combine the flour, thyme, sage, tarragon, salt, and pepper in a large mixing bowl; dredge the chicken pieces in the seasoned flour.

Fill a large skillet with oil about ¼-inch deep and heat the oil to 350 degrees. Place the chicken in the hot oil and cook in batches until golden brown on all sides and until the interior temperature has reached 180 degrees, about 10 to 12 minutes per side. Add more oil as needed.

Remove the chicken pieces from the pan and drain them on a sheet pan or wire rack for 5 to 10 minutes before serving.

To prepare the cream gravy:
In a large saucepan, melt the butter and sauté the chicken livers and onion for 2 minutes.

Slowly stir in the flour, wine, stock or broth, and cream.

Increase the heat to high and bring to a boil, stirring constantly; reduce the heat to low and simmer for 15 minutes.

Puree the gravy in a blender, strain, and return it to the pan. Add salt and pepper to taste. Heat until warmed through and serve.

Lamb

4 to 6 lamb hind shanks

Salt and freshly ground black
    pepper to taste

4 tablespoons grape seed oil
    or canola oil, divided

1 cup diced onion

2 carrots, peeled and chopped

2 celery stalks, chopped

1 tablespoon minced fresh rosemary
    (or 1 teaspoon dried)

2 teaspoons chopped fresh thyme
    leaves (or ½ to ¾ teaspoon
    dried)

¼ cup tomato paste

Salt and freshly ground black
    pepper to taste

1½ cups red wine

4 cups lamb, veal, or chicken stock

Gremolata

¼ cup finely minced flat-leaf parsley

3 garlic cloves, finely minced

Zest of 2 lemons

Makes 4 to 6 servings

Lamb Ossobucco

OLIVER'S BAR AND GRILL, SHERIDAN
OWNER/CHEF OLIVER "MATT" WALLOP

*A favorite at the restaurant, this popular Italian dish is served with
Tuscan-Style Beans (see the recipe in the Salads and Sides section) and
garnished with gremolata, a traditional Italian accompaniment.*

To prepare the lamb:
Preheat the oven to 300 degrees. Season the shanks liberally with salt
and pepper.

In a Dutch oven, arrange the shanks in a single layer. Do not over-
crowd the pan; cook in batches if necessary. Heat the pan over
high heat until it is nearly smoking, then add 2 tablespoons of oil.
Decrease the heat to medium and cook the meat until it is evenly
browned on all sides. Transfer to a deep platter so the juices can
collect and the meat can rest.

Remove the darkened bits and excess oil from the pan; add the
remaining 2 tablespoons of oil, onion, carrots, and celery to the pan
and sauté over medium heat until lightly browned.

Stir in the rosemary, thyme, and tomato paste; continue cooking over
medium heat until the tomato paste begins to brown.

Add more salt and pepper and the red wine. Cook for 5 minutes over
medium-high heat, stirring frequently to deglaze the pan.

Place the shanks in a single layer over the vegetables and add enough
stock to nearly cover the shanks, leaving one-quarter of the lamb
exposed at the top. Cover with a tightly fitting lid, lower the heat,
and simmer for 5 minutes.

Transfer to the oven and bake for 3 hours, or until fork-tender. Remove from the oven, keep covered, and let rest for 30 minutes.

To prepare the gremolata:
Combine the parsley, garlic, and lemon zest in a small mixing bowl. Do not prepare ahead; the gremolata tastes best when fresh.

Presentation:
Arrange a mound of beans in the center of dinner plates or bowls. Carefully remove each lamb shank from the pan and place over the beans. Ladle about ½ cup of the cooking liquid over the shanks and sprinkle with gremolata.

PUBLISHED IN *SOME CHURCH*
BY MILKWEED EDITIONS IN 2005

"WINTER ROOTS"
BY DAVID ROMTVEDT, WYOMING'S STATE POET LAUREATE

Long winter and the parsley waits with the rhubarb and iris,
the dog who lies on his back by the fire, his legs splayed out
and rising above him like roots upside down plunged into the sky.
Suspended from clouds in dream. Time to rest.

But those who would shape the world in their image do not rest—
the generals and governors, the presidents and prime ministers,
the surgeons and priests, the schoolteachers planning their next test,
the policemen bent over pulling weeds, those unconscious resisters.

Some green soul comes up wondering if it might be spring,
buds nipped by an ice storm, snow piling up on the spinach and kale.
Kale, a word that sounds like kill or keel or coal, the earth guarding
its fire, waiting, as stone and water, as you and I, dormant and pale.

4 (5-ounce) trout fillets

Salt and freshly ground black
    pepper to taste

½ cup whole milk

1 cup all-purpose flour

4 tablespoons clarified butter

2 tablespoons butter

2 tablespoons coarsely
    chopped hazelnuts

¼ cup lemon juice

2 tablespoons freshly chopped
    flat-leaf parsley

Makes 4 servings

In 1872, President Ulysses Grant signed a law creating Yellowstone National Park—not only the first national park in the United States, but the first in the world. The Old Faithful Inn, built from 1903 to 1904, is one of the few remaining original log hotels in the country. This grand hotel features lodgepole pine walls and ceiling beams, a giant volcanic rock fireplace, and green-tinted windows etched with scenes from the 1920s. In 1915 and 1927, wings containing additional rooms were added to this magnificent inn, and today it is the most popular place to stay in the park.

Pan-Fried Rocky Mountain Trout with Hazelnut Butter

YELLOWSTONE NATIONAL PARK HISTORIC RECIPE, JULY 25, 1934

Imagine the pleasure of fishing for trout in the park's remote streams that wind through flowering meadows surrounded by the towering pines and majestic mountains fringed in snow. This historic entrée continues to delight guests who dine in the park lodges. I like to serve this dish with Marinated Asparagus (see the recipe in the Salads and Sides section). A note on the butter used in this recipe: Clarified butter is unsalted butter that has had the milk solids and water removed so all that remains is the butter fat. It is produced by melting the butter to allow the components to separate.

Wash the trout fillets and pat them dry. Season both sides of the fillets with salt and pepper.

Pour the milk into a shallow, wide bowl and coat the fillets with milk. Dredge the milk-coated fillets in flour and set aside.

In a large skillet, heat the clarified butter over medium heat; sauté the fillets in the butter, turning them only once, until cooked to the desired doneness. Remove them from the pan and keep warm.

Dispose of the remaining clarified butter in the pan and add the whole butter. Melt the butter over medium heat until slightly browned.

Add the hazelnuts, stirring constantly, and cook until lightly toasted.

Stir in the lemon juice and parsley, heat through, and serve over the warm trout.

Marinade

2 tablespoons olive oil

1 tablespoon minced garlic

1 tablespoon minced shallots

2 tablespoons freshly chopped
    rosemary

1 tablespoon black peppercorns

3 bay leaves

1¾ cups dry sherry

1 cup soy sauce

½ cup water

Duck breasts

4 boneless duck breasts
    (2 whole breasts, halved and
    trimmed with skin intact)

2 to 3 tablespoons canola oil

Makes 4 servings

Roast Duck Breast with Apple and Sun-Dried Cranberry Chutney

THE BLUE LION RESTAURANT, JACKSON   ❧   CHEF TIM LIBASSI

The marinade is prepared a day ahead so the duck breasts can marinate overnight. All that is left to do is roast the duck and make the chutney. I like to serve this dish with Scalloped Sweet Potatoes (see the recipe in the Salads and Sides section) for a stunning holiday dinner.

To prepare the marinade:
Heat the oil in a small saucepan and sauté the garlic, shallots, rosemary, peppercorns, and bay leaves for 3 to 4 minutes.

Add the sherry, soy sauce, and water; bring to a boil to burn off the alcohol.

Remove from the heat and transfer to a 13 x 9 x 2-inch baking dish. Refrigerate to cool.

To prepare the duck breasts:
Make three to four slits in each duck breast and lightly pound them to flatten.

Place the breasts in the marinade, cover with plastic wrap, and refrigerate overnight, turning once.

Preheat the oven to 425 degrees. Heat the oil in a large skillet over medium-high heat; remove the duck breasts from the marinade and sear them skin-side down until crispy.

Turn and sear the other side for 1 minute and transfer to a roasting pan. Roast skin-side down to preferred doneness. Remove from the oven and let rest for 10 minutes before slicing.

Chutney

4 tablespoons butter

½ red onion, chopped

3 celery stalks, chopped

2 tablespoons minced garlic

2 tablespoons minced ginger

½ cup brandy

½ cup dry red wine

¾ cup rice vinegar

2¼ cups apple juice

2 pounds tart cooking apples,
    peeled, cored, and chopped

1 cup sun-dried cranberries

½ cup brown sugar

1 teaspoon ground cinnamon

1 teaspoon ground nutmeg

1 teaspoon ground coriander

1 teaspoon ground thyme

½ teaspoon cloves

¼ teaspoon ground allspice

To prepare the chutney:
Melt the butter in a saucepan and sauté the onion, celery, garlic, and ginger until the onion is translucent.

Stir in the brandy, red wine, rice vinegar, and apple juice; cook over medium-high heat until reduced by 75 percent.

Add the apples, cranberries, brown sugar, cinnamon, nutmeg, coriander, thyme, cloves, and allspice; cover and simmer over low heat until the chutney is thick and warmed through, about 20 to 25 minutes.

Presentation:
Spread even amounts of chutney on four warm dinner plates; place each duck breast skin-side up in the center of each plate over the chutney.

Cod

4 (6-ounce) black cod fillets
(about 1½ pounds)

4 tablespoons vegetable oil

Salt and white pepper to taste

Stewed tomatoes

4 vine-ripened tomatoes

2 tablespoons olive oil

1 teaspoon chopped garlic

1 teaspoon chopped fresh basil

Sauce

4 tablespoons butter

¼ cup all-purpose flour

2 cups light chicken stock or broth

2 cups heavy cream

½ head cauliflower, cut into
small florets

Salt and white pepper to taste

4 teaspoons white truffle oil

Makes 4 servings

Roasted Black Cod with Stewed Vine-Ripened Tomatoes, Cauliflower Sauce, and White Truffle Oil

YELLOWSTONE NATIONAL PARK
EXECUTIVE CHEF JAMES CHAPMAN

For this delectable entrée, prepare the stewed tomatoes and cauliflower sauce first and keep them warm while the cod is baking. The tomatoes can be made a day ahead and reheated, but do not add the basil until you are ready to serve the dish.

To prepare the cod:
Preheat the oven to 400 degrees. Coat each fillet on both sides with 1 tablespoon of oil. Season with salt and pepper and bake for 10 minutes.

To prepare the stewed tomatoes:
Peel, seed, and chop the tomatoes.

In a medium saucepan, heat the olive oil and sauté the garlic over medium heat for about 5 minutes. Avoid browning.

Add the tomatoes and reduce the heat to low. Simmer the tomatoes until they are tender and most of the liquid has evaporated, about 15 minutes, or to desired consistency.

Stir in the basil before serving.

To prepare the sauce:
In a small saucepan, melt the butter over medium–low heat and stir in the flour with a fork to make a roux. Cook for 3 minutes, remove from the heat, and let cool.

In a medium saucepan, combine the stock or broth, cream, and cauliflower. Bring to a boil over high heat; reduce the heat to low, cover, and simmer until the cauliflower is soft, about 15 minutes.

Remove from the heat and cool slightly before pureeing in a blender or food processor.

Return the mixture to the saucepan and whisk in the roux over low heat. Bring to a low boil, add salt and pepper to taste, and remove from the heat.

Pass the sauce through a fine strainer, return to the pan, and keep warm while the cod is baking.

Presentation:
Spoon an even amount of sauce in the center of four warm dinner plates. Place the cod on top of the sauce, spoon a dollop of stewed tomatoes over the cod, and drizzle 1 teaspoon of truffle oil over each serving.

Wyoming family picnic. WYOMING STATE ARCHIVES, DEPARTMENT OF STATE PARKS AND CULTURAL RESOURCES, MEYERS NEG 1708A

Scallops, spinach, and carrots

4 tablespoons canola oil, divided

16 sea scallops (U-10 scallops recommended)

½ cup lardons (small dice, thick-cut bacon)

1 pound baby spinach leaves

2 jumbo carrots, peeled and julienned

Kosher salt

Citrus beurre blanc

8 tablespoons butter (1 stick)

2 tablespoons lime juice

1 cup white wine

1 tablespoon chopped shallots

1 bay leaf

1 garlic clove, sliced

Makes 4 servings

Sea Scallops with Frizzled Spinach, Carrots, and Citrus Beurre Blanc

WILD SAGE RESTAURANT AT RUSTY PARROT LODGE AND SPA, JACKSON ✺ EXECUTIVE CHEF JEFFREY BLACKWELL

The Wild Sage Restaurant is one of only a few distinctive restaurants in Wyoming and Montana to earn the prestigious AAA Four Diamond designation. Light and pretty, this imaginative entrée is ideal for spring and summer dinners. The chef recommends preparing the beurre blanc sauce first and reheating immediately before serving.

To prepare the scallops, spinach, and carrots:
Heat 2 tablespoons of oil in a deep skillet over high heat and sear the scallops in batches for 2 to 3 minutes, or until golden brown; turn and cook for 2 minutes. Add more oil as needed. Remove the scallops from the pan and keep warm.

Discard the oil from the pan and add the bacon and spinach; cook quickly over high heat to frizzle, or make crispy. Remove from the pan and keep warm.

Heat the remaining oil over high heat to 300 degrees. Cook the carrots until crispy. Remove the carrots from the oil and drain on a platter lined with paper towels. Sprinkle with kosher salt and set aside.

To prepare the citrus beurre blanc:
Cut the butter into 1–inch cubes and chill.

In a medium saucepan, combine the lime juice, wine, shallots, bay leaf, and garlic; cook over medium heat until reduced by 90 percent.

Remove from the heat and slowly add the butter, one cube at time, stirring constantly and gently.

Presentation
Evenly distribute the frizzled spinach and bacon mixture onto the center of warm dinner plates; arrange four scallops on top. Drizzle the sauce around the scallops and top with crispy carrots.

Tenderloin

4 (6- to 8-ounce) elk tenderloins

Salt and freshly ground black
    pepper to taste

2 tablespoons butter

Port wine sauce

1 pound assorted fresh mushrooms

3 tablespoons butter

1 cup port wine

1¾ cups veal or beef stock

1 tablespoon cornstarch
    dissolved in 2 tablespoons
    water (optional)

Makes 4 servings

Seared Elk Tenderloin with Port Wine Sauce

THE GRANARY RESTAURANT AT SPRING CREEK RANCH, JACKSON
EXECUTIVE CHEF JASON MITCHELL

Paired with Winter Root Vegetable Hash (see the recipe in the Salads and Sides section), this is one of the most popular entrées at the award-winning Granary Restaurant.

To prepare the tenderloins:
Preheat the oven to 400 degrees. Rub salt and pepper on both sides of the tenderloins.

Coat a large skillet with butter and heat over medium–high heat; sear the tenderloins on both sides, about 1 to 2 minutes for each side.

Transfer to a shallow rack in a roasting pan and roast to preferred doneness (for medium–rare, internal temperature is 126 to 130 degrees).

To prepare the wine sauce:
Clean and slice the mushrooms.

In a large saucepan, sauté the mushrooms in the butter over medium–high heat until tender. Remove the mushrooms from the pan with a slotted spoon and set aside.

Add the port wine to the pan and cook over medium–high heat until reduced by 75 percent, about 5 to 7 minutes.

Stir in the stock. If a thicker sauce is desired, stir in the cornstarch. Cook over medium–high heat until bubbly.

Gently fold the sautéed mushrooms into the sauce and remove from the heat.

Tenderloin

1 (4-pound) beef tenderloin, washed and dried

4 garlic cloves, minced

4 tablespoons coarsely ground black pepper

¾ cup Worcestershire sauce

1 ½ cups soy sauce

1 ⅓ cups beef stock or broth

Mushroom-Roquefort sauce

¼ pound Roquefort cheese

½ cup butter

3 garlic cloves, minced

1 tablespoon Worcestershire sauce

¼ teaspoon caraway seeds

½ cup chopped green onions, including tops

½ pound button mushrooms, sliced

Makes 6 to 8 servings

In 1906, President Theodore Roosevelt declared Devils Tower the country's first national monument. This magnificent vertical monolith is also known as Bears Lodge, and it is a sacred site for many local Native American tribes.

Trappers Peak Tenderloin with Mushroom-Roquefort Sauce

DEVILS TOWER LODGE, DEVILS TOWER

An old family recipe of the lodge proprietor, this entrée is a guest favorite. I like to serve it with Roasted Garlic Mashed Potatoes and Marinated Asparagus (see the recipes in the Salads and Sides section).

To prepare the tenderloin:
Rub the tenderloin with the minced garlic and black pepper.

Combine the Worcestershire and soy sauces in a baking dish; marinate the beef for 3 hours at room temperature.

Preheat the oven to 500 degrees.

Discard the marinade and pour the stock or broth around the beef; transfer to the oven and reduce the heat to 350 degrees. Cook the tenderloin for 18 minutes per pound for rare or 20 minutes per pound for medium–rare. Remove from the oven and let rest for 15 minutes before slicing.

To prepare the sauce:
In a medium saucepan, combine the cheese, butter, garlic, Worcestershire sauce, and caraway seeds; cook over low heat until the cheese and butter are melted.

Add the onions and mushrooms. Cook, stirring constantly, for 2 to 3 minutes.

2 cups fresh French green beans

2 teaspoons butter

½ cup sliced almonds

2 whole trout fillets

2 tablespoons olive oil

1½ teaspoons chopped fresh
    flat-leaf parsley
    (or ¾ teaspoon dried)

¾ teaspoon chopped fresh thyme
    (or ½ teaspoon dried)

1½ teaspoons lemon juice

Salt and freshly ground black
    pepper to taste

Makes 2 servings

Trout Almondine

TRIO, JACKSON
OWNERS/CHEFS WILL BRADOF, BEAU LITTLE, AND PAUL WIREMAN

I love trout, and this recipe makes the best of it! Simply double the ingredients to prepare additional servings.

Bring 4 cups of water with a pinch of salt to a boil and add the green beans. Bring the water back to a boil and cook for 2 to 3 minutes, until the green beans are crisp-tender. Drain the green beans and rinse with cold water to halt the cooking; set aside.

Melt the butter in a small saucepan and cook the almonds over medium heat until golden, stirring constantly, about 5 minutes. Remove from the heat and set aside.

Preheat the oven to 500 degrees. Rinse the trout fillets and pat them dry. Season the sides of the trout with salt and pepper.

Heat the olive oil in a large oven-safe sauté pan over high heat until smoking and place trout skin-side down in pan. Cook for 3 to 4 minutes; pour off the excess fat and add the green beans.

Transfer to the oven and bake the trout for 4 minutes; remove from the oven. Place one piece of trout skin-side down on a dinner plate, top with 1 cup of green beans, and place another piece of trout on top. Repeat for the second serving.

Using the same pan, heat the butter over high heat and add the browned almonds. As the butter begins to slightly brown and foam, add the parsley, thyme, and lemon juice. Season with salt and pepper and pour over the trout. Serve immediately.

(See photograph on page 71)

Brisket

4 pounds beef brisket

1 teaspoon celery salt

1 teaspoon garlic salt

1 teaspoon onion salt

1 tablespoon Worcestershire sauce

Dash liquid smoke (optional)

Sauce

½ cup chopped onion

½ cup ketchup

½ cup water

¼ cup cider vinegar

4 tablespoons butter

2 tablespoons lemon juice

2 tablespoons Worcestershire sauce

2 tablespoons sugar

1 tablespoon prepared mustard

1 ½ teaspoons salt

1 teaspoon black pepper

¼ teaspoon cayenne pepper

Makes 8 to 12 servings

Wrangler's Brisket

FLYING A RANCH, PINEDALE

The secret to making a great brisket is to cook it over low heat for a long period of time, and this recipe does just that. If pressed for time, use your favorite prepared barbecue sauce. Serve with Roosevelt Beans and Colorful Cabbage Salad (see recipes in the Salads and Sides section) for an authentic Western meal.

To prepare the brisket:
Preheat the oven to 275 degrees. Place the beef in a Dutch oven or roasting pan; sprinkle evenly with the celery salt, garlic salt, onion salt, Worcestershire sauce, and liquid smoke, if desired. Cover and refrigerate overnight.

Bake the brisket for 5 to 6 hours, or until fork-tender. Remove from the oven and cool to room temperature. Transfer to the refrigerator and cool for 1 hour before slicing.

To prepare the sauce:
Combine the onion, ketchup, water, vinegar, butter, lemon juice, Worcestershire sauce, sugar, mustard, salt, black pepper, and cayenne pepper in a medium saucepan and bring to a low boil; lower heat and simmer for 30 minutes.

Preparation:
Preheat the oven to 350 degrees. Remove the brisket from the refrigerator and trim the excess fat. Slice the beef against the grain and layer the meat in a large oven-safe glass baking dish or baking pan. Pour the sauce over the beef and cover with aluminum foil; bake for 45 minutes, or until warmed through.

4 beef short ribs

Salt and freshly ground black
    pepper to taste

2 to 3 tablespoons olive oil

1 onion, peeled and diced

1 carrot, peeled and diced

2 celery stalks, chopped

1 tomato, chopped

24 ounces Zonker or
    Guinness Stout

4 cups beef stock or broth

1 tablespoon minced garlic

8 sprigs fresh thyme

2 bay leaves

Makes 2 to 4 servings

Zonker Stout Braised Short Ribs

GAMEFISH RESTAURANT AT SNAKE RIVER LODGE AND SPA,
JACKSON HOLE   ℞   EXECUTIVE CHEF KEVIN HUMPHREYS

Zonker Stout is a dark beer brewed in Jackson at the Snake River Brewing Company. You may substitute with a comparable stout beer such as Guinness. Beer has tenderizing properties, making it an excellent marinade for tougher cuts of meat, and it adds rich flavor.

Preheat the oven to 250 degrees. Season the short ribs with salt and pepper on all sides.

Heat the oil in an oven-safe pan over medium-high heat and brown the short ribs evenly.

Remove the ribs from the pan and add the onion, carrot, and celery. Cook the vegetables over medium heat, stirring occasionally, until lightly browned.

Stir in the tomato and cook for 2 minutes, stirring frequently.

Add the beer, stock or broth, garlic, thyme, and bay leaves; lower the heat and simmer.

Return the short ribs to the pan, cover, and bake undisturbed for 3½ hours. Remove the ribs from the pan and keep warm.

Strain the liquid into a saucepan; cook over medium-high heat, stirring frequently, until the sauce is reduced to a thick consistency. Skim the sauce to remove fat as needed; remove the thyme sprigs and bay leaves. Add salt and pepper to taste.

Desserts & Sweet Treats

Wild Huckleberry Muffins with Orange Glaze, p. 116

Filling

4 cups fresh or frozen huckleberries

1 cup sugar

2 tablespoons all-purpose flour

¼ cup Chambord liqueur (optional)

Topping

1 cup bread flour

½ cup sugar

½ cup brown sugar

½ cup toasted chopped pecans

½ cup melted butter (1 stick)

1 teaspoon vanilla extract

1 teaspoon cinnamon

¼ teaspoon nutmeg

½ teaspoon salt

Makes 6 to 8 servings

Huckleberries are a favorite food
of many animals, including bears.
Small in size and varied in color,
huckleberries may range from tart
to sweet in taste, with a flavor
similar to blueberries.

Berry Crisp

EARTH AND VINE, JACKSON
EXECUTIVE CHEF TIM PAYNE AND SOUS CHEF JAIME RUSSONIELLO

*This rustic crisp is made with fresh huckleberries at the bistro, but you
may substitute with raspberries, blackberries, or blueberries for variation.
The addition of Chambord, a French black raspberry liqueur, gives this
delightful dessert a rich, deep flavor. I like to serve it warm with a scoop
of vanilla ice cream.*

To prepare the filling:
In a large mixing bowl, combine the berries, sugar, flour, and liqueur,
if using. Pour the mixture into a lightly oiled cast-iron skillet or
8 x 8-inch baking pan and set aside.

To prepare the topping
Preheat the oven to 350 degrees. Combine all of the ingredients in a
large mixing bowl and sprinkle over the berry mixture. Bake for 25
to 30 minutes, or until the topping is golden brown.

1 sheet frozen puff pastry,
    thawed in refrigerator

1 cup heavy cream

1 cup chopped semisweet
    dark chocolate

2 eggs, yolks only

2 teaspoons cocoa powder
    (optional garnish)

Makes 12 servings

Built in 1888 by Erasmus Nagle,
the Nagle Warren Mansion
is one of Cheyenne's most
elegant residences. In 1910, Francis
Warren—a businessman who
served as Wyoming's first state
governor and one of the state's
first United States senators—
purchased the property. It is now
a beautiful bed-and-breakfast that
has been refurbished to re-create
the Victorian elegance of the
Old West.

Bittersweet Chocolate Tart

NAGLE WARREN MANSION BED AND BREAKFAST, CHEYENNE

At the mansion, the tart shell is homemade; however, I've adapted the recipe using frozen puff pastry to save time in preparation. Cut the tart into small wedges and serve them on dessert plates sprinkled lightly with cocoa powder.

Preheat the oven to 425 degrees. Unfold the cold pastry and, on a lightly floured surface, roll it into a 12-inch square.

Gently place the pastry into a 9 x 1-inch round tart pan, being careful not to stretch or tear the dough. Trim the pastry and gently press it into the tart pan edges; using a fork, lightly prick several holes in the dough.

To keep the dough from puffing, lightly oil the underside of a 9-inch glass pie dish and place it into the tart pan on top of the dough.

Bake for 20 minutes, or until lightly golden. Remove from the oven, remove the glass pie dish, and cool for 30 minutes.

In a medium saucepan, warm the cream over low heat. Stir in the chocolate and cook until the chocolate is melted, stirring frequently to avoid scorching. Remove from the heat.

Whisk the egg yolks in a separate mixing bowl and slowly add them to the chocolate mixture, mixing until creamy and smooth. Fill the baked tart shell with the chocolate mixture, cover with plastic wrap, and refrigerate 4 hours or overnight.

Remove the tart from the refrigerator and bring to room temperature before serving. Cut the tart into wedges and place on serving plates; sprinkle with cocoa powder if desired.

½ cup raisins

¼ cup dark rum

8 cups day-old Texas toast bread,
    cut into 1-inch cubes

4 cups heavy cream

3 eggs

1⅔ cups sugar

1 tablespoon vanilla extract

¼ cup melted butter

1 cup whipped cream
    (optional garnish)

½ cup maple syrup
    (optional garnish)

Makes 12 servings

Bread Pudding

CM RANCH, DUBOIS ❧ CHEF AMY BEAN

An old-fashioned favorite, this bread pudding is a crowd-pleaser. At the ranch, it is served with whipped cream or a drizzle of pure maple syrup. Either way, it is sure to delight your family and guests.

Preheat the oven to 350 degrees. In a small saucepan, combine the raisins and rum. Simmer over low heat for 5 minutes, cover, and set aside.

Place the bread in a large mixing bowl and cover it with the cream; set aside and allow the bread to absorb the cream.

Whisk together the eggs, sugar, and vanilla extract in a small mixing bowl. Stir in the warmed rum, raisins, and melted butter. Combine with the bread cubes and spread in a lightly buttered baking dish.

Bake for 45 minutes, or until golden brown and set. Serve warm, topped with whipped cream or pure maple syrup.

4 eggs

2 cups sugar

¾ cup melted butter (1½ sticks)

2 teaspoons vanilla extract

1½ cups all-purpose flour

½ teaspoon baking powder

¼ teaspoon salt

⅓ cup cocoa

3 milk chocolate Hershey Bars,
finely chopped

3 Reese's Peanut Butter Cups,
chopped

1 cup chopped walnuts

Candy Bar Brownies

VEE BAR GUEST RANCH, LARAMIE

These magical brownies are fun to make with the kids. I recommend you prepare two batches since they will vanish quickly! For variation, substitute with other favorite standard-size candy bars in the same amounts listed.

Preheat the oven to 350 degrees. In a large mixing bowl, combine the eggs, sugar, butter, and vanilla extract; beat until smooth with an electric mixer.

In a separate mixing bowl, combine the flour, baking powder, salt, and cocoa. Sift the dry ingredients into the egg mixture and mix well.

Fold in the chopped candy and pour the mixture into a lightly oiled and floured 13 x 9 x 2-inch baking pan.

Bake for 30 to 35 minutes. Remove from the oven and cool slightly before cutting into the desired number of bars.

1 cup butter at room temperature

1 cup brown sugar

½ cup sugar

1 tablespoon molasses

1 tablespoon almond extract

2 eggs

3 cups ground quick-cooking oats
    (grind oats in food processor)

1 ½ cups all-purpose flour

1 teaspoon baking soda

½ teaspoon salt

1 cup craisins (dried cranberries)

½ cup chopped walnuts

Makes about 36 to 42 cookies

Craisin-Walnut Oatmeal Cookies

SPOTTED HORSE RANCH, JACKSON HOLE
CHEF AARON STUMP

These traditional cookies are dressed up with almond extract, ruby-red craisins, and crunchy walnuts. For variety, substitute vanilla extract for almond extract and chocolate chips for craisins.

Preheat the oven to 375 degrees. Using an electric mixer, beat the butter, sugars, molasses, and almond extract until smooth.

Beat in the eggs one at a time and whip the mixture for 2 to 3 minutes on high speed.

In a separate mixing bowl, whisk together the ground oats, flour, baking soda, and salt.

Add the butter mixture to the dry mixture and combine until smooth. Stir in the craisins and walnuts.

Drop the dough by heaping tablespoons onto a lightly oiled cookie sheet. Bake for 10 minutes, or until the edges are golden brown and the cookies are soft to the touch. Remove from the oven and let rest for 5 minutes before transferring to racks to cool.

4 apples, cored, peeled,
   and diced

2 cups dark rum

4 eggs, separated

1¼ cups sugar

8 tablespoons butter at room
   temperature (1 stick)

1 cup plus 1 tablespoon
   all-purpose flour

1½ teaspoons baking powder

Makes 6 to 8 servings

The TA Guest Ranch was home-
steaded in 1884 and had only four
previous owners in more than
120 years. The initials "TA" on the
ranch's brand—among the earliest
brands registered in Wyoming—
belong to Tom Alsop, who started
a herd outside Laramie while
helping supply Union Pacific rail-
building crews in the early 1880s.

El's Rum Cake

TA GUEST RANCH, BUFFALO

*Named for a former ranch employee from Belgium, this is one of many
signature offerings at the ranch that proprietors Barbara and Earl Madsen
have collected over the years.*

Marinate the apples and rum in a glass dish overnight.

Preheat the oven to 350 degrees.

Combine the egg yolks and sugar in a large bowl. Add the butter,
flour, and baking powder and beat until smooth, using an electric
mixer. Gently fold the apples and rum marinade into the mixture
and set aside.

In a separate mixing bowl, beat the egg whites just until they begin
to stiffen and form peaks; gently fold into the cake mixture.

Pour into a 9-inch springform cake pan and bake for 50 minutes.

¾ cup sugar

¼ cup cornstarch

Dash salt

2 eggs

¼ cup water

2 cups milk

1 teaspoon vanilla extract

1 cup shredded coconut

1 (9-inch) ready-made crumb
    crust or baked pie shell

1 cup whipped cream

Makes 1 (9-inch) pie

Goldie's Coconut Cream Pie

TEA KETTLE RANCH BED AND BREAKFAST, TORRINGTON
ISABEL HOY

Given to innkeeper Isabel Hoy when she was a young bride in 1964 by a neighboring rancher's wife named Goldie, this special cream pie recipe has endured the test of time. Isabel uses a ready-made pie shell, but if you want to make yours from scratch, see the basic pie crust recipe featured with the Sour Cream Cherry Pie recipe in this section. Topped with whipped cream, this pie is an old-fashioned, melt-in-your-mouth treat.

Combine the sugar, cornstarch, and salt in a mixing bowl and set aside.

In a separate bowl, whisk the eggs and water.

Heat the milk in a double boiler or saucepan until just scalding. Pour the eggs and water mixture into the milk and beat slightly with a wire whip. Stir in the dry ingredients and mix well. Cook over medium heat, stirring constantly, until the mixture is thick and just begins to bubble. Stir in the vanilla extract and coconut and remove from the heat.

Let the mixture cool for 20 minutes, stirring occasionally. Pour the filling into the pie shell and refrigerate for at least 1 hour before serving. Top with whipped cream when ready to serve.

3 ounces chopped white chocolate

2 cups whole milk

½ teaspoon vanilla extract

Grated nutmeg or chocolate
  sprinkles for garnish

Makes 2 servings

Heavenly Hot Chocolate

THE WILDFLOWER INN, JACKSON HOLE

At the inn, this dreamy beverage is also made with coffee; simply add one-third cup brewed coffee for a delicious variation. Use a high-quality white chocolate to yield a creamier, richer flavor.

Combine the chocolate and milk in a small saucepan and cook over low heat to melt the chocolate, stirring frequently, being careful not to burn. Add the vanilla extract and cook over medium heat, stirring constantly. Pour into mugs and sprinkle with grated nutmeg or chocolate sprinkles.

2 ½ cups all-purpose flour

1 ¼ cups sugar

3 teaspoons cinnamon

2 teaspoons baking soda

½ teaspoon salt

3 eggs

¾ cup applesauce

½ cup canola oil

1 teaspoon vanilla extract

2 cups grated carrots

1 tart apple, peeled, cored, and grated

1 cup crushed pineapple, drained

½ cup flaked coconut

½ cup raisins

½ cup chopped walnuts

Makes 24 muffins

Morning Glory Muffins

CASPER MOUNTAIN BED AND BREAKFAST, CASPER

What a glorious assortment of ingredients in these lively muffins! They taste best when served warm. I enjoy mine with a smidgen of honey and a hot cup of English breakfast tea.

Preheat the oven to 350 degrees. In a large mixing bowl, combine the flour, sugar, cinnamon, baking soda, and salt.

In a separate mixing bowl, whisk together the eggs, applesauce, oil, and vanilla. Pour this into the flour mixture and stir until moistened (batter will be thick). Stir in the carrots, apple, pineapple, coconut, raisins, and walnuts.

Pour the batter into lightly oiled standard-size muffin tins (or use paper muffin cups), two-thirds full. Bake for 20 to 25 minutes. Let rest for 5 minutes before removing from pans.

Mountain Mud Slide

HOTEL WOLF, SARATOGA

2 tablespoons Kahlúa

2 tablespoon Bailey's Irish Cream

2 tablespoons amaretto

⅓ cup half-and-half

4 scoops vanilla ice cream

½ cup whipped cream

Makes 2 servings

Built in 1893, the Hotel Wolf opened with an elaborate dinner and gala masquerade ball on New Year's Eve. Listed on the National Register of Historic Places, the hotel has been beautifully restored to its original charm. Top this delightful dessert drink with grated chocolate for a chic presentation.

Combine the Kahlúa, Bailey's Irish Cream, amaretto, half-and-half, and ice cream in a blender and mix until creamy. Pour into serving glasses and top with whipped cream.

Skiing the old-fashioned way. COLLECTION OF THE JACKSON HOLE HISTORICAL SOCIETY AND MUSEUM, 1993.4942.001

2 cups baking mix

2 eggs

½ cup milk

½ cup sugar

1 teaspoon vanilla extract

¼ cup canola oil

½ cup semisweet chocolate chips

½ cup fresh or frozen raspberries

Makes 12 muffins

Raspberry-Chocolate Chip Muffins

IVY HOUSE INN, CASPER

Chocolate and raspberries make the perfect pair, and these divine muffins are a lovely treat to serve on Valentine's Day or during the holidays.

Preheat the oven to 400 degrees. In a large mixing bowl, combine the baking mix, eggs, milk, sugar, vanilla extract, and oil. Gently fold in the chocolate chips and raspberries.

Lightly oil a standard-size muffin tin or line one with paper cups; fill with batter three-quarters full. Bake for 20 to 25 minutes until golden brown and the tops spring back when touched.

PUBLISHED BY THE PENGUIN GROUP IN 1986

FROM *THE SOLACE OF OPEN SPACES* BY GRETEL EHRLICH

Despite the desolate look, there's a coziness to living in this state. There are so few people (only 470,000) that ranchers who buy and sell cattle know one another statewide; the kids who choose to go to college usually go to the state's one university, in Laramie; hired hands work their way around Wyoming in a lifetime of hirings and firings. And despite the physical separation, people stay in touch, often driving two or three hours to another ranch for dinner.

Crust

1 cup all-purpose flour

½ cup butter

5 tablespoons powdered sugar

Pinch salt

Filling

2 eggs, beaten

1½ cups sugar

¼ cup all-purpose flour

¾ teaspoon baking powder

3 cups diced fresh or frozen rhubarb

Makes 6 servings

Rhubarb Torte

FLYING A RANCH, PINEDALE

Rhubarb, a perennial vegetable plant that originated in Asia, was probably brought to Wyoming by emigrants from the eastern United States in the mid-1800s. Because rhubarb is a cool-season crop, it is popular among Wyoming gardeners, who use it in cakes, pies, pastries, jams, sauces, pickles, and wine.

To prepare the crust:
Preheat the oven to 375 degrees. In a mixing bowl, combine the flour, butter, powdered sugar, and salt.

Lightly oil a 9 x 9 x 2-inch baking pan and pat the ingredients into the pan to form a crust on the pan bottom. Bake for 10 to 12 minutes, or until golden brown.

To prepare the filling:
In a large mixing bowl, combine the eggs, sugar, flour, baking powder, and rhubarb. Pour over the partially baked crust and bake for 35 to 40 minutes.

Filling

1 cup all-purpose flour

1¼ cups plus 2 tablespoons sugar

¼ teaspoon salt

1 cup sour cream

3 cups fresh or frozen pitted
    tart cherries

Basic pie crust

1 ½ cups all-purpose flour

½ teaspoon salt

½ cup chilled shortening

1 tablespoon butter

3 tablespoons ice water

Makes 1 (9-inch) pie

Sour Cream Cherry Pie

THE SPOKE CAFÉ, MEETEETSE

This sweet, creamy pie may be prepared with fresh or frozen strawberries, raspberries, rhubarb, or peaches for variation. Topped with whipped cream or ice cream, this is a luscious dessert that is easy to prepare, especially if you use a ready-made, unbaked pie shell.

To prepare the filling:
Preheat the oven to 450 degrees. Sift the flour, 1¼ cups of the sugar, and the salt together in a large mixing bowl. Gently stir in the sour cream and cherries; mix well.

Spread the mixture into a deep 9-inch pie shell and sprinkle the remaining sugar over the top. Bake for 10 minutes, then reduce the temperature to 325 degrees and bake 30 minutes longer, or until the filling is baked through and the crust is light golden brown.

To prepare the pie crust:
In a medium-size mixing bowl, sift together the flour and salt. Add the shortening and butter. Using a fork or pastry cutter, combine into a coarsely crumbled mixture. Gradually add the ice water and mix well.

Shape the dough into a ball and cover with plastic wrap. Refrigerate for at least 30 minutes.

When chilled, roll the dough out on a lightly floured surface and gently place in a 9-inch pie pan; trim the edges and press the sides into the pan using thumb and forefinger.

With a population of just 351, Meeteetse (*muh-TEET-see*) is one of the oldest settlements in the Bighorn Basin and has an intriguing history. Legend has it that outlaws Butch Cassidy and the Sundance Kid, along with other members of the Hole-in-the-Wall Gang, frequented the town's drinking and dining establishments in the late 1800s. The town's distinctive name is said to derive from a Shoshone or Arapaho phrase meaning "meeting place." Literally translated, Meeteetse means "measured distance near and far."

Ten Sleep Tea

2 cups water

2 chamomile tea bags
(or 2 tablespoons chamomile
tea leaves)

2 tablespoons apple brandy

2 teaspoons honey

Pinch allspice

Pinch cinnamon or cinnamon stick

Makes 2 cups

Ten Sleep, population 315,
is located on the western slope
of the Bighorn Mountains. It was
named by American Indians who
stopped there to rest after ten days
of travel, or "ten sleeps," from Fort
Laramie, Yellowstone National
Park, and the Indian Agency on
the Stillwater River in Montana.

*I concocted this soothing hot tea tonic following an excursion to the
enchanting little village of Ten Sleep, nestled at the base of the Bighorn
Mountains about thirty miles from my home. Substitute apple cider for
brandy if you prefer a non-alcoholic version of this relaxing tea.*

Heat the water to a low boil. Combine the tea, brandy, honey,
allspice, and cinnamon in a teapot and add the hot water. Steep
for 5 minutes and serve.

Muffins

½ cup butter

¾ cup sugar

2 eggs

1 cup plain yogurt

¼ cup sour cream

2½ cups all-purpose flour

1 tablespoon baking powder

½ teaspoon baking soda

¾ cup huckleberries or blueberries

Glaze

1 cup powdered sugar

¼ cup half-and-half

Zest of 1 orange

Candied orange zest (optional garnish)

Zest of 1 orange

1 cup sugar

½ cup water

Makes 12 muffins

Wild Huckleberry Muffins with Orange Glaze

THE ALPINE HOUSE, JACKSON ✦ CHEF ERIC BARTLE

A Scandinavian-style inn built with century-old timber beams, the Alpine House is a warm, inviting bed-and-breakfast located in the heart of Jackson that serves the best breakfasts I have ever tasted. Blueberries or cranberries may be substituted for huckleberries in these scrumptious muffins. Garnish with candied orange zest for a pretty presentation.

To prepare the muffins:
Preheat the oven to 350 degrees. In a large bowl, use an electric mixer to beat the butter and sugar until smooth and creamy. Slowly add one egg at a time, mixing on low speed. Gradually add the yogurt and sour cream.

In a separate mixing bowl, combine the flour, baking powder, and baking soda; slowly add to the liquid ingredients with the mixer on low speed.

Gently fold the berries into the mixture and pour into oiled muffin tins, filling each tin three-quarters full. Bake for 20 minutes, or until light golden brown.

To prepare the glaze:
Combine the sugar, half-and-half, and orange zest in a mixing bowl and drizzle over the warm muffins.

To prepare candied orange zest:
Combine the sugar and water in a small saucepan and bring to a boil over high heat, stirring frequently. Reduce the heat to low and stir in the orange zest. Cook for 5 to 10 minutes, or until reduced to a thick syrup. Arrange 1 to 2 tablespoons on top of each muffin and allow to set for 5 minutes before serving.

(See photograph on page 99)

2 cups of your favorite
vanilla ice cream

¼ cup vanilla flavoring

Makes 1 to 2 servings

Yellowstone Drug Store Vanilla Shake

YELLOWSTONE DRUG STORE, SHOSHONI

In the early 1900s, Shoshoni was a bustling town with a population of nearly 2,000. During the boom time, there were a number of thriving businesses, including twenty-three saloons and the Yellowstone Drug Store, which has endured for over a century, serving tens of thousands of malts and shakes each year. This legendary soda fountain is located in a building once owned by C. H. King, grandfather of former President Gerald Ford. For flavored shakes, simply substitute another flavoring or fruit and blend with vanilla ice cream.

Combine the ice cream and flavoring in a blender and serve immediately.

sources for specialty ingredients and other products

Azure Standard is an online organic grocery store that sells quality natural products. http://www.azurestandard.com/index.php

Belle Cose is a specialty store located in downtown Jackson featuring fine tableware, cookware, kitchen tools, linens, and home accessories. http://www.bellecose.com

Cameron Ranch is a Wyoming working ranch that produces high-quality grass-fed beef and lamb. Their livestock are raised in a natural, stress-free environment. http://cameronranch.com/index.html

Club Sauce is a premier website that sells an array of gourmet products, including demi glace, stocks, vinegars, oils, condiments, seasonings, and other specialty ingredients. Expert food tips, articles, cookbooks, and food links are also provided. http://clubsauce.com

Gateway Gourmet is an excellent website for gathering information on how to prepare superior sauces. Tips for preparing soups and stews are also provided. http://www.gatewaygourmet.com

Grande Premium Meats sells USDA North American elk, bison, venison, and beef. Alaskan salmon and halibut are also available at their website. http://www.elkusa.com/index.html

igourmet.com is a unique online specialty store that features fine food products from around the world. http://igourmet.com

Jackson Hole Buffalo Meat Company has a store located in Jackson where you may purchase bison, elk, smoked trout, and gourmet gift products. These items are available on their website as well. http://www.buybuffalomeat.com

Mexgrocer.com offers an assortment of authentic Mexican food products, including achiote paste and a variety of peppers. http://www.mexgrocer.com

Nature's Cuisine is an online store with a variety of wood cooking planks, recipes for cooking on planks, and other unique cooking products.

Wyoming First is a showcase for a variety of products made in Wyoming. It is my favorite source for chokecherry and huckleberry jams. http://www.wyomingfirst.org

contributors

Alpenrose Restaurant at the Alpenhof Lodge
3255 West Village Drive
Teton Village, WY 83025
(800) 732-3244 or (307) 733-3242
http://www.alpenhoflodge.com

The Alpine House
285 North Glenwood Street
Jackson, WY 83001
(800) 753-1421 or (307) 739-1570
http://www.alpinehouse.com

Altitude Chophouse and Brewery
320 South Second Street
Laramie, WY 82070
(307) 721-4031
http://www.altitudechophouse.com

The Blue Lion Restaurant
160 North Millward Street
Jackson, WY 83001
(307) 733-3912
http://www.bluelionrestaurant.com

The Bunnery
130 North Cache
Jackson, WY 83001
(307) 734-0075
http://www.bunnery.com

Cameron Ranch
7325 Riverview Road
Riverton, WY 82501
(307) 856-6057
http://cameronranch.com

Casper Mountain Bed and Breakfast
4471 South Center
Casper, WY 82601
(307) 237-6712
http://www.caspermountainbnb.com

CM Ranch
Post Office Box 217
Dubois, WY 82513
(800) 455-0721 or (307) 455-2331
http://www.cmranch.com

Devils Tower Lodge
Devils Tower, WY 82714
(888) 314-5267 or (307) 467-5267
http://www.devilstowerlodge.com

Earth and Vine
260 West Pearl Street
Jackson, WY 83001
(307) 734-5033

Fire Rock Steakhouse and Grill
6100 East Second Street
Casper, WY 82609
(307) 234-2333
http://www.firerocksteakhouse.com/begin.html

Flying A Ranch
771 Flying A Ranch Road
Pinedale, WY 82941
(888) 833-3348 or (307) 367-2385
http://www.flyinga.com

Gamefish Restaurant
at Snake River Lodge and Spa
7710 Granite Loop Road
Teton Village, WY 83025
(307) 732-6050
http://snakeriverlodge.rockresorts.com

The Granary Restaurant
at Spring Creek Ranch
1800 Spirit Dance Road
Jackson, WY 83001
(800) 443-6139 or (307) 733-8833
http://springcreekranch.com

Grand Victorian Lodge
85 Perry Street
Jackson, WY 83001
(800) 584-0532 or (307) 739-2294
http://www.grandvictorianlodge.com

The Historic Plains Hotel
1600 Central Avenue
Cheyenne, WY 82001
(866) 275-2467 or (307) 638-3311
http://www.theplainshotel.com

Hotel Wolf
101 East Bridge Street
Saratoga, WY 82331
(307) 326-5525
http://www.wolfhotel.com

The Howdy Pardner Bed and Breakfast
1920 Tranquility Road
Cheyenne, WY 82009
(307) 634-6493
http://howdypardner.net

The Irma Hotel
1192 Sheridan Avenue
Cody, WY 82414
(800) 745-4762 or (307) 587-4221
http://www.irmahotel.com

Ivy House Inn
815 South Ash Street
Casper, WY 82601
(307) 265-0974
http://www.ivyhouseinn.com

Jenny Lake Lodge
Grand Teton National Park
Moran, WY 83013
(800) 628-9988 or (307) 733-4647
http://www.gtlc.com/lodgeJen.aspx

Lovejoy's Bar and Grill
101 Grand Avenue
Laramie, WY 82070
(307) 745-0141
http://www.elmerlovejoys.com

Nagle Warren Mansion Bed and Breakfast
222 East Seventeenth Street
Cheyenne, WY 82001
(800) 811-2610 or (307) 637-3333
http://www.naglewarrenmansion.com

Oliver's Bar and Grill
55 North Main Street
Sheridan, WY 82801
(307) 672-2838

The Pines Restaurant at Teton Pines Resort
and Country Club
3450 North Clubhouse Drive
Wilson, WY 83014
(800) 238-2223 or (307) 733-1005
http://www.tetonpines.com

Porch Swing Bed and Breakfast
502 East Twenty-fourth Street
Cheyenne, WY 82001
(307) 778-7182
http://www.cruising-america.com/porchswing/
porch.html

Ranger Creek Guest Ranch
3261 Paintrock Road
Shell, WY 82441
(254) 241-6022
http://www.rangercreekranch.net

Red Rock Ranch
Post Office Box 38
Kelly, WY 83011
(307) 733-6288
http://www.theredrockranch.com

Remington's Restaurant
at the Powder Horn Golf Clubhouse
23 Country Club Lane
Sheridan, WY 82801
(307) 673-0001
http://www.thepowderhorn.com/clubhouse.html

Rendezvous Bistro
380 South Broadway
Jackson, WY 83002
(307) 739-1100
http://www.rendezvousbistro.net

Shadows Brewing Company
115 West Fifteenth Street
Cheyenne, WY 82001
(307) 634-7625
http://www.snakeriverpub.com

The Spoke Café
1947 State Street
Meeteetse, WY 82433
(307) 868-2110

Spotted Horse Ranch
12355 South Highway 191
Jackson Hole, WY 83001
(800) 528-2084 or (307) 733-2097
http://www.spottedhorseranch.com

Sweetwater Restaurant
85 King Street
Jackson, WY 83001
(307) 733-3553
http://restauranteur.com/sweetwater

TA Guest Ranch
28623 Old Highway 87
Buffalo, WY 82834
(307) 684-5833
http://www.taranch.com

Tea Kettle Ranch Bed and Breakfast
9634 Van Tassell Road
Torrington, WY 82240
(307) 532-5375
http://www.wyomingbnb-ranchrec.com/
teakettle.html

Trio
45 South Glenwood Street
Jackson, WY 83001
(307) 734-0054
http://bistrotrio.com

Vee Bar Guest Ranch
2091 State Highway 130
Laramie, WY 82070
(800) 483-3227 or (307) 745-7036
http://www.veebar.com

Waldorf A'Story
at Piney Creek General Store
19 North Piney Road
Story, WY 82842
(307) 683-2400
http://www.pineycreekgeneralstore.com

The Wildflower Inn
3725 Teton Village Road
Jackson, WY 83001
(307) 733-4710
http://www.jacksonholewildflower.com

Wild Sage Restaurant
at Rusty Parrot Lodge and Spa
175 North Jackson Street
Jackson, WY 83001
(888) 739-1749
http://www.rustyparrot.com

Yellowstone Drug Store
127 Main Street
Shoshoni, WY 82649
(307) 876-2539

Yellowstone National Park Lodges
Operated by Xanterra Parks and Resorts
Post Office Box 165
Yellowstone National Park, WY 82190
(866) 439-7375 or (307) 344-7311
http://www.travelyellowstone.com

Dave and Nancy Freudenthal, Wyoming's governor
and first lady, Cheyenne

Jim and Sherri Geringer, Wyoming's former governor
and first lady, Wheatland

Former U.S. Senator Alan Simpson
and Ann Simpson, Cody

index